9221-312-4
Congress: 95-72880

Multnomah Graphics, Portland, Oregon

ıre references, unless otherwise indicated are taken from the
ɛ, New International Version, copyright 1973, 1978, 1984 by
ıal Bible Society. Used by permission of Zondervan Publishing

graphs in this book were obtained exclusively from Historic
s, 2150 Central Avenue, Augusta, GA 30904. These photo-
ı the early superstars up to the present day. Framed prints make
ions to any home, office, or clubhouse. For ordering informa-
 (706) 737-3062.

Lesson from t Fairw

by
R. McKenzie

New Leaf Press

First pri

Copyrig
United S
in any m
except in
tion writ

ISBN: 0-
Library

Cover by

All Scrip
Holy Bib
Internatic
House.

The phot
Golf Prir
graphs sp
great add
tion phon

Presented to:

_____

Presented by:

_____

Date:

_____

Dedication

The more of these All-Star Moments we write, the longer the list of people who have contributed to their success. For the sake of brevity, many of you must go unnamed, but I do want to give special thanks to the following people:

Ed — for his love and especially for rescuing me when the computer crashed!

Brian — for proofreading my manuscripts. (He's a better writer than I am.)

Mom — for being so brave after breaking her wrist. (You were *not* a bother!)

Eve — for sharing her knowledge of the publishing industry and for her special friendship.

Larry Nelson— for his willingness to write our Foreword and for his example on the PGA Tour. Also to Larry Moody for making the contact for us and to Greg Stoughton and others at Athletes in Action for their terrific "networking."

The Clermont County Public Library (Milford) staff—for making my research as painless as possible. (What great timing for the installation of their new computer system! No fines for several months! PTL!)

Everyone at New Leaf — for their patience over the holidays when I was supposed to be writing.

And as always, Jesus for the LAF (love, acceptance, and forgiveness) that brings peace to my soul even in these hectic times.

Foreword

Rita Fisher offers a wonderful compilation of stories and actual golf tips in *Lessons from the Fairway* — a mixture from professionals and amateurs, from men and women, from history and current events, from club pros to the weekend hackers.

That is the wonderful thing about the game of golf. It can be truly anyone's game. The couple or family who plays a scramble together can have just as much fun as those of us on the PGA tour. Without all the pressure and media coverage, you all might enjoy it more. However, I doubt that. I don't know any professional who is out here playing strictly for the money and the prestige. We all truly love the game.

Golf is also a game that you can play for a lifetime, as Rita suggests in "Seasoned Golfers." Golf is a game that is good for us mentally, physically, and socially. It encourages us to concentrate. It provides fellowship and time for friendships to deepen — and for business relationships to develop into friendships. It teaches us manners and respect for one another. Of course, it also offers a great way to exercise. Even if you must ride a cart, you walk to your ball and from putt to putt (unless you're like Ben Crenshaw and one-putt a lot). Walking is one of the best forms of exercise, and there's no better place to walk than in God's great outdoors.

There's no better person to walk with than God. Golf courses have some of the most beautiful scenery on earth. I will admit that I am most often concentrating on my next shot as I walk the fairway rather than conversing with God. But sometimes, even I the midst of some of the most important tournaments I've played, I have suddenly felt His presence in the wonder of His creation.

The best thing about walking with Christ is that it doesn't make any difference what kind of weather we have. On the windiest day, when the storms of life are hitting all around us, He is there beside us. He may not always still the wind, but He can still our hearts and keep us at peace. There are other times, when things are going well, that we need to remind ourselves that He is walking with us — and providing the joys we are celebrating.

I know that for my family, walking with Jesus has meant more joy and peace. I hope you all find some joy and fun in reading the lessons in this book.

I also hope you will share it with others. The book makes a wonderful gift for anyone you know who likes the game of golf. Christian friends will enjoy the connections I mentioned earlier. If you have golfing friends who do not know Christ, this little gift book may be the very connection to Him they need. While you may not feel comfortable talking with them about their relationship with God, you can make the approach by giving them a copy of *Lessons from the Fairway*. They certainly will not be offended by the lessons and it may make all the difference in their lives.

Accepting Christ and getting to know Him better has made all the difference in mine.

Larry Nelson
PGA Tour Pro

Introduction

Golf has been a family sport for us from the beginning. I learned to play while in junior high school, and Ed and I played a lot after we were first married. Later, with my doctor's approval, I was still playing two weeks before Brian was born.

Ed adapted our stroller into my golf cart by using larger wheels on the back and mounting black plastic club tubes between the handle and the bottom of the basket in back. Brian's bottles, diapers, and a few toys went in the basket and the canopy provided his shade.

As soon as he could toddle around, we bought him one of those sets with the softball-sized plastic ball and big yellow plastic driver. Ed had to cut the blue handle down to Brian's height. He would get in his practice swings off the greens or while we waited on a tee. Gradually we changed his ball and club(s) to regulation size.

When my allergies aren't too severe, we still all play together. Brian plays for "real" — aiming for birdies and pars. Ed has a successful round if he finds more balls in the woods than he loses. I just play for the exercise and fellowship and prefer scrambles where I can hit from someone else's "best ball."

One personal highlight came while Brian and I (and a whole horde of other fans) walked 18 holes with Michael Jordan at Boomer Esiason's celebrity golf tournament to benefit Juvenile Diabetes. Only once did Jordan drive a ball well into the rough and he encouraged everyone to help him find it. Much to all of the kids' chagrin, I located it first. When MJ said, "Thanks, Mama," I replied, "No problem, I'm used to finding my balls in this part of the course!" (Actually, I'm hoping some of the research for this book might improve my game!)

Speaking of research — Brian noticed I quote Harvey Penick and Nancy Lopez quite often in the following lessons. I was somewhat more limited in sources this time. There were more books available for researching baseball and football. Since we also hope to involve women more in this book, Nancy's was the only one I found written from a women's perspective, so I do tend to quote her a lot. As for Harvey, there just isn't a better instructor. His books are filled with SO much great information! (You really need to read them all.) I also want to apologize to all "southpaws." All the golf books I read give instructions for right-handed golfers only. You will need to read the lessons in reverse. (You might want to call 1-800-844-NALG or 6254 for the National Association of Left-Handed Golfers.) How frustrating it must be for all of you! At least it gives you an excuse. I basically understand all of the lessons and still play most shots out of the rough.

My suggestion for the title of this book was either *Lessons from the Tee* or *Lessons from the Green* since some of us seldom see the fairways. (Maybe even *Lessons from the Rough* or . . . *the Trap* — you get the picture of my game.) Whatever the level of your game and from wherever you walk to play your shots, I hope you enjoy the game as much as our family. Moreover, I hope the connections we make in this book will bring you a lasting kind of joy and peace in Christ. A daily walk with Jesus is the best life can offer!

In His love,
Rita McKenzie Fisher

Lesson 1

Perfection

Never had the U.S. Open Golf Tournament begun with such a fanfare! Immediately after the trumpet blast to start play on June 12, 1980, Tom Watson sank a hole in one off his opening tee! Golf at its perfection!

Shooting a hole in one means everything works as it should — the swing, accuracy, distance — and a little luck! Yet even a hole in one does not a winner make. Jack Nicklaus won the 1980 Open, not Tom Watson.

To most non-professional golfers an even-par round on a regular basis would be perfection, but golf is not a game of perfection.

Al Geiberger came as close as anyone, shooting one of the only two rounds of 59 ever scored on the PGA tour. He shot his 59 in the Danny Thomas Memphis Classic in 1977. Chip Beck also shot a 13-under-par 59 in the third round of the Las Vegas Invitational in 1991.

Geiberger has watched a lot of young players enter the professional ranks. "They will be playing great for six or seven holes and then they hit one bad shot, and then they hit bad shots the rest of the round because they're expecting perfection." Geiberger suggests, "You have to have an attitude in golf that you won't have perfection."

If you understand that concept, it may save you a lot of heartache and dejection. British golf star Nick Faldo shares, "There isn't a lonelier place in all of sport than the golf course when things aren't going your way. You're basically on your own out there. You can't call your local professional for a lesson. You can't get the video camera out for a look at

9

your swing. And all the while the ball just sits there looking at you, waiting for your next move."

Life itself can be lonely, especially when our sins just sit there looking at us. Life isn't perfect, and neither are we! No matter how hard we try, we continue to make mistakes because we are limited in power and wisdom.

"Everything of human origin has its limits and end; but the commands of God are boundless," says Ron Auch in his devotional commentary on Psalm 119 entitled *The Heart of the King.* Auch tells us why our perfection is limited: "Man's problem is that he often tries to accomplish the will of God through his own means." Auch continues, "But we need to be dependent on God."

The Bible tells us that "all have sinned and fall short of the glory of God" (Rom. 3:23). But we can call on God to save us from our dejection and despair. All we have to do is come to Him with honest and humble hearts. Ask His forgiveness through the blood that His only Son shed for us and commit our lives to Jesus Christ. When we put our limits behind and come to Christ, at that point God's limitless commands take over and accomplish what we never could.

Our only claim to perfection is in following Him.

"If we confess our sins, he is faithful and just and will forgive us our sins and purify us from all unrighteousness" (1 John 1:9).

"Golf is a game you cannot perfect. You'll hit some great shots, but in fact it's really a game of misses — a game of how good your misses are."
— Al Geiberger

Lesson 2
Seeing Is Believing

Great golfers don't worry, "I've got to avoid that bunker," or "Look out for those trees on the left." They think "target" on every shot!

At age eight, Tiger Woods already understood and used this philosophy. Asked what he was thinking about on the first tee of one of his earliest tournaments, young Tiger responded, "Where I wanted the ball to go." Perhaps that's why by age 11 he was undefeated in 30 junior events.

Woods also began watching tapes of former Masters tournaments at age six. Watching (and imitating) great players is another way of training your "mind's eye" to develop a good golf swing.

Al Geiberger helped develop a visualization lesson series entitled *Neuromuscular Training for Golf*. The video portion has no voice lessons — only repetitions of the smooth, effective swings of Geiberger.

Gary Player also visualizes. He says, "On a chip, have a clear picture of the whole shot. See the spot where it lands and see it roll into the hole." Tom Kite calls it making "a map in your mind" or "a mental image of the type of shot you want to play and where you want the ball to end up." Jack Nicklaus called it "going to the movies" in your own head. Nancy Lopez says, "Almost every top player I know does this for every shot."

The high handicapper probably doesn't make a mental picture of any shot. He takes a vague sort of aim and tries to clobber the ball. If you can "see" the shot, your muscles will do their best to make it happen.

In the Foreword of his book *Visual Golf,* Ken VanKampen says: "I visualize every shot, whether it's a drive, approach, chip, or putt. Even when I step up to tap a 12-inch putt, I make sure to run the image of the ball dropping into the cup through my head."

The same holds true in other aspects of life as well. As VanKampen says of golf, "The more clearly you can envision what you want to do, the better your chances of doing it."

You can take any situation and do a dress rehearsal in your mind that will let you handle yourself more confidently. What is happening in your life? Do you need to give a speech, control your temper, quit smoking, limit your drinking, propose to your girlfriend, tell your parents you are moving? Do a "mental rehearsal." Close your eyes and watch yourself reacting calmly rather than screaming angrily when your two year old spills her milk.

You can also "see yourself" in Bible stories as an exciting way to study Scriptures. Can you imagine yourself like Peter, walking on the water toward Jesus, or sitting on the hillside as Christ delivers his Sermon on the Mount, or witnessing the crucifixion from the nearby crowd at Calvary? See yourself as one of the disciples as Jesus explains your favorite parable. You can even see (and feel) Christ as He reaches out to embrace you with His unconditional love.

"For as he thinks within himself, so he is" (Prov. 12:7).

"In my mind's eye, I can let myself see the entire shot, from beginning to end. I even try to imagine how the swing will feel."
— Nancy Lopez

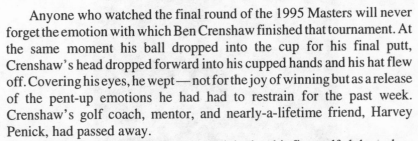

Lesson 3

Mentors

Anyone who watched the final round of the 1995 Masters will never forget the emotion with which Ben Crenshaw finished that tournament. At the same moment his ball dropped into the cup for his final putt, Crenshaw's head dropped forward into his cupped hands and his hat flew off. Covering his eyes, he wept — not for the joy of winning but as a release of the pent-up emotions he had had to restrain for the past week. Crenshaw's golf coach, mentor, and nearly-a-lifetime friend, Harvey Penick, had passed away.

Penick had watched as Crenshaw picked up his first golf club as a boy of six or seven and continued to instruct him right to the end. Crenshaw had visited the last Sunday in March, and even though Harvey was ill in bed, he had Ben get the old wooden putter from the garage so they could check his grip. Harvey's son, Tinsley, would give Crenshaw that same putter as a gift after the funeral less than two weeks after that final visit. Crenshaw, along with tour friend and another Penick devotee, Tom Kite, left the practice rounds of the Masters to fly to Austin mid-week to be pallbearers at their dear mentor's funeral.

Crenshaw certainly felt Penick's spirit during the tournament. Donning the green jacket awarded to the Masters' Champion, an emotional Ben said, "I'll never know how I got through. I had a 15th club in my bag. It was Harvey." (Players are permitted to carry only 14 clubs throughout a tournament.)

Ben Crenshaw
1995 Master's Winner

While Penick enjoyed watching his students win on tour, he still enjoyed helping the average golfer. Improving someone's game so he wouldn't embarrass himself during a business round, or teaching a woman how to play the game so she and her husband could enjoy a round together, was truly a blessing to Harvey. He often said he "got goose bumps just from the joy of being able to help." Harvey loved the game, loved people, and loved life itself. He shares all three with guru-like wisdom found in the golfing volumes he finally agreed to write — especially *The Little Red Book*.

How many of us get similar "goose bumps" from helping others? Isn't this the call of true discipleship to Christ — to reach out to others around us with love, understanding, and help?

Think of those who have been mentors in your life. When and how did they reach out to you? Give them a call or write them a note of appreciation. What are the valuable lessons you learned from them? How are you sharing those with others? Whom might God want you to mentor — maybe in some athletic endeavor or another area of life?

Jesus was a prime example of mentoring. What else would you call what He did with the Twelve? In Christian circles, it is referred to as "discipling" and it didn't stop with Jesus. Paul became a mentor to Timothy, as did Barnabas to John Mark. New Christians need the loving acceptance and wisdom of more mature believers to help "disciple" them. Do you have a Christian mentor — someone more mature you can turn to for advice and loving confrontation when you need it? You may be called on to disciple a believer newer than yourself.

What qualities are needed for discipling? First we must be committed to Christ and follow His example. We need to be self-disciplined in study, worship, and prayer. We should be empathetic and understand where others are in their spiritual walks and not expect them to be where we are or where we might want them to be.

Whom is God calling you to disciple?

"The pleasantness of one's friend springs from his earnest counsel. As iron sharpens iron, so one man sharpens another" (Prov. 27: 9, 17).

[On what Penick's death meant to Crenshaw]: "It was like losing his dad and his best friend at the same time." — Davis Love III (lost to Crenshaw by one stroke in the 1995 Masters)

Lesson 4
A Historical Perspective

The game of golf may date back to cavemen smacking at pebbles with their clubs, or shepherds like those in the hills of Bethlehem striking stones with their crooks. Roman legionnaires in the days of Caesar played a similar game called paganica with clubs and leather balls filled with feathers.

However, the modern game we know began in the 15th century with the Scottish who laid out green links along their shorelines. They also determined the rules for the game, which basically remain intact today. In 1457 King James II of Scotland banned golf because he was concerned that it was becoming so popular that it might interfere with archery which was a part of the national defense. When James VI acceded to the English throne as James I, he took his golf clubs along and the game became quite popular. Mary, Queen of Scots, also loved the game and encouraged women to play as well. St. Andrews, where the British Open is sometimes played, was established in Edinburgh in 1744. The Inaugural Open was begun in 1895. Women (through the Ladies Golf Union) began tournament play about the same time. In 1893 Lady Margaret Scott won the first of her three LGU titles.

Golf had also come to the "other side of the pond" (across the Atlantic Ocean). Walter Hagen is considered by most to be the first professional golfer in America and helped start the PGA in 1916. He toured from 1914-1929 and, along with the popular amateur Bobby Jones, dominated the sport in the 1920s. Joyce Wethered was considered the top female golfer in that decade, but women's golf lagged behind men's play until after World War II. The LPGA was established in 1948 and the feminist movement of the 1960s also furthered women's golf. Patty Berg and Betty Jameson helped give the LPGA its start, but a true "star" was born when Babe Didrikson Zaharias (famed Olympic winner) came to the tour.

Others who helped increase the popularity of golf through the years have been Ben Hogan, Sam Snead, Arnold Palmer, Jack Nicklaus, Tom Watson, and a host of dynamic young players on the PGA Tour today. Likewise, Mickey Wright, JoAnne Carner, Pat Bradley, Judy Rankin, Kathy Whitworth, and others helped develop the LPGA Tour, along with Nancy Lopez and other current players.

Non-professionals also helped popularize the game. President Dwight Eisenhower enjoyed the game (as have most presidents since) and even had a putting green built on the White House grounds.

We study history (whether golf, national, or spiritual) not just to appreciate our ancestry, not just to build upon the premises of individuals from the past, not just to learn and hopefully avoid similar mistakes. We also become an actual part of history itself.

Local Methodist pastor Fred Shaw, unlike most of us who read the Bible, loves the genealogies and can tell the story of Christ's birth through His lineage. Shaw says, "All the saints who went before us brought us to this place." He also challenges us to "celebrate that God works in human lives like ours to change the world." Shaw reminds us that "we are the next step in eternity."

While we study the forefathers of our faith in the Bible, our response to what we read and to God's grace in our own lives is writing new chapters for ourselves and our families that will be a part of eternity.

What part of eternity are you?

"God has also set eternity in the hearts of men; yet they cannot fathom what God has done from beginning to end" (Eccles. 3:11).

"The game is essentially the same as it was in 1895 when 11 men strode to the first tee at the inaugural Open." — Brett Avery (editor of *Golf Journal*)

Lesson 5
How's Your Grip?

You can tell a lot about a person from his or her handshake. Is it firm or weak? The same can be said of one's "grip" on the golf club. How you hold it will say a lot about what kind of player you are.

Harvey Penick, one of the world's best golf instructors, began his lessons by asking students to let their arms hang naturally at their sides. "It would be unusual to stand with your palms out, so just fit the club gently into your left hand and grip it." Your left thumb will be slightly to the right, not straight on the shaft so that your hands will fit together smoothly as one working unit.

Bring the club in front of you and as Harvey suggests, "Extend your right hand out as if to shake hands, and place it on the club below your left hand." Your right hand should be parallel to the shaft of the club — "like aiming a pistol" according to Nancy Lopez, but with your forefinger wrapped gently around the club.

You can snug the right hand next to the left hand with all ten fingers touching the club for the baseball grip. However, many advanced golfers prefer either the overlap or interlock grip. For an overlap (or Vardon) grip, the little finger of your right hand overlaps the forefinger (actually fits in the crevice between the forefinger and middle finger) of your left hand.

With the interlock grip (especially good for people with short fingers), these same two fingers are entwined rather than over-lapped. Because we get more "feel" with our fingers, use your fingers as much as possible rather than the palm of your hands. Choose the grip that feels most comfortable for you. It is a personal preference.

The "V" made between the thumb and forefinger of each hand is a key in making the proper grip. Your left-hand "V" should point toward your right shoulder. If this "V" goes too far left, you will have a weak grip and get a hard-to-correct slice (left to right movement on the ball); if too far right, this is too strong and will cause a terrible hook (right to left). With the proper grip and the club positioned in front of you, Penick says "You should see three knuckles of the left hand." If only 2 or 2-1/2 knuckles are showing, you have not made the proper turn on your grip. Check that left "V."

How tightly should you hold the club? Sam Snead always said to hold the club like a little bird: "Tight enough it can't get away, but loose enough that he can breathe." Lopez says she imagines holding a tube of uncapped toothpaste so that the paste doesn't come squirting out all over. Penick warns, "Your elbows and shoulders should feel relaxed. Grip firmly, but not tightly."

This is good advice for our "spiritual grip" as well. We must hold firmly to the convictions of our faith, but we should not be so rigid on non-essential matters that we become like the Pharisees, who Christ most often chastized.

We can crush the Holy Spirit of new believers by insisting they follow the exact interpretations that we have come to hold. Remember, like our golf grip, faith needs to be personal. We cannot insist someone else automatically assume our beliefs. If they do, they will not be truly their own, and confession to God and commitment to Christ must be done on a one by one basis. We must each have a personal faith to hold on to.

Jesus said, "If you hold on to my teaching, you are really my disciples. Then you will know the truth, and the truth will set you free" (John 8:31-32).

"Imagine a clock with the shaft at twelve o'clock. Your left "V" should be at 1:00 and your right one at 11:00." — Ben Alexander (co-director of golf instruction at Pebble Beach)

Lesson 6
"I've Got Rhythm"

Grip. Stance. Ball position. Aim. Now we're ready to swing the club. Many players begin with a "waggle" — one or two short movements back and forth (or up and down) of the club to "get the adrenaline flowing" or "start the motor." A slight forward press (maybe even cocking the right knee a bit) can be the action that causes a reaction (being your backswing).

Your legs begin the swing, followed by your torso and your arms. Too many amateurs swing with their arms only. Tom Kite explains that when the legs begin to move, the action centers in your lower back. He suggests picturing a line of skaters rotating in a large circle. The skater at the center moves very slowly making a small circle, but the people at the ends must skate faster and make a much wider circle on the ice. Even though the outer skaters are moving faster, it is the inside person who controls the speed. "The big muscles of your back don't have the range of motion that your arms do," says Kite. "They don't have to because they are turning at the center of your swing."

As you shift your weight onto the right leg (and side), you begin the take back with the club. Keep your arms and wrists straight (not stiff) and continue until the club shaft is parallel with the ground. As your arms and the club come back down and you strike the ball, your body weight will automatically shift to your left leg. Extend your arms and the club for a full high follow-through. Remember to keep your eyes on the ball during the complete swing.

Jack Nicklaus
The Bear

Watch any of the great golfers. You will see fluid, smooth swings. That is the key. For most individuals, that also means a slow rhythm. Al Geiberger says, "There is only one fast moment in every swing." You want to accelerate on the downswing to make that moment at impact. If your take away is too hard or fast, your momentum ends up at the top of your swing and you actually decelerate as you swing through the ball. Harvey Penick says, "Store up energy going back and release that energy coming forward. It's just like throwing a punch or a baseball, or like the serve in tennis."

Your tempo, how fast or hard you swing, needs to be correct for you; but the slower the better for most players. Former President Gerald Ford could swing a club almost as fast as Jack Nicklaus, but all of Ford's speed was on the backswing. Nicklaus has said when he wants to hit the ball farther, he takes the club away even more slowly.

Swinging faster and hitting a ball harder can mean less accuracy. Nancy Lopez reminds us hitting the ball 10 to 20 yards further isn't any advantage if it means playing from a deeper part of the rough. "A poorly hit shot, when hit hard, only means you're deeper into the woods," she says. "Be careful if you play with someone whose tempo is much different than yours," warns Lopez. "Don't get into their game." You may begin copying their tempo without even realizing it. Maintain your own rhythm.

Also stick with your own approach routine. After selecting your club, you may want to take a practice swing or two. (Some professionals do; some don't.) Then look down your target line. Focus (and visualize) where you want your shot to go. Check your ball (or place it on the tee). Get into your stance. Use your "wagggle," and begin your smooth, fluid swing.

Make certain to follow-through. Keep your personal routine the same every time.

Our daily routines often have the same problems as our golf swings — the tempo is too rushed. We are always in a hurry and often make mistakes by speeding ahead without thinking. We do not like to wait in lines, for loved ones to get ready, or for answers to prayer. We are an impatient people.

"Patience must be rooted in an overarching confidence that there is Someone in control of this universe, our world, and our life." says pastor and author Lloyd John Ogilvie. "A patient person knows the shortness of time and the length of eternity. Patience is really faith in action."

"The end of a matter is better than its beginning, and patience is better than pride" (Eccles. 7:8).

"Let the inner circle control the outer circle!" — Tom Kite

Lesson 7
Take Dead Aim!

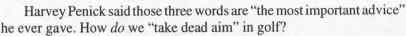

Harvey Penick said those three words are "the most important advice" he ever gave. How *do* we "take dead aim" in golf?

Imagine a straight line running through the tee (or where your ball is positioned) and directly to your target. Assume your normal address. Also imagine a second line running directly in front of your feet. These two imaginary lines should be parallel to one another. With both hands horizontally in front of you, grasp your club and let it come to rest across your thighs. Where does the club point? If your feet are aligned properly, the club should point slightly left of your target (since you are standing behind the actual target line).

Nancy Lopez says the reason most golfers hit the ball to the right is because they aim their body (not the ball) at the target. She warns, "Your body should be parallel to the target line, not aimed at the target."

If you consistently hit your shots either to the right or the left, make certain your clubface comes through the ball squarely at impact. Penick advises, "To see where on your clubface you're hitting the ball, powder the ball at the driving range. Look for the powder on the face." If that does not correct the problem, you may want to make SLIGHT adjustments in your stance.

To "fade" the ball (so it will start left and fade back right), move only your left foot slightly back from your imaginary toe line. This is called an "open stance" and causes an outside-in spin as the clubface strikes the ball along the imaginary target. Be careful not to over-correct or you will hit an uncontrollable "slice."

For the opposite adjustment or to "draw" the ball (so it will start right and come back left), begin again with the straight alignment but move only your right foot back slightly. This is a "closed stance" and causes you to strike the ball from the inside-out. An over-adjustment in this area can cause an ugly "hook."

Some instructors suggest making adjustments in your grip. However, most winning players do not tinker with a successful and comfortable grip. Corey Pavin says, "As for changes to my regular method, I try to keep it simple. I keep the grip the same and change the alignment of the clubface," which is done by opening or closing one's stance. Pavin's hint: "You aim the body toward where the ball begins and the clubface toward where you want the ball to end."

Use these same adjustments in aiming for specific areas of the fairway or on doglegs (where the fairway makes a turn before reaching the green). Another key for doglegs or long holes is to pick out intermediate targets along an imaginary line between the tee and the hole. Aim directly for one of these shorter targets. Tom Watson makes another dogleg suggestion. He moves to the opposite edge of the teeing area to "help straighten out the hole." He says "playing a dogleg is like driving a car around the corner. You want the smoothest, safest route — the most efficient."

Most of us would like to be more efficient in our daily lives as well. We must "take dead aim" — setting goals and priorities so we don't waste time. In teaching how to keep a spiritual journal, Ronald Klug makes several suggestions about setting goals. Assess where you are and how you spend your time. We must be realistic and know we can't do everything. We must make choices. Set short-term goals that lead to completed projects (intermediate targets). Create a balance of work, play, and worship. Klug warns us that without goals and priorities, we tend to "fall into what is easiest and most urgent rather than what is most important."

Klug quotes Henri Nouwen as saying, "If you don't control your own time, according to the will of God as you see it, others will control your time for you."

"Trust in the Lord with all your heart and lean not on your own understanding; in all your ways acknowledge him, and he will make your paths straight" (Prov. 3:5-6).

[When making any adjustments] "Always make small changes, don't over-do it. When the doctor says take aspirin, he doesn't mean the whole bottle." — Harvey Penick

Lesson 8
What's Your Address?

Once you feel comfortable with your grip, what's next? First of all —
RELAX! You're going to "address the ball." Tee your ball up at a
comfortable distance from your body. Your arms should be extended and
straight, but never stiff and rigid, with your elbows relaxed — neither
locked nor bent.

Your stance should also be comfortable. The taller you are, the wider
your stance needs to be to stay in proper balance. Off the tee and for longer
clubs, you will need a shoulder-wide stance. As you move to the shorter
distance clubs, your stance will automatically narrow. Some exceptions
are made on specialty shots (Lesson 26.). You want your feet basically
parallel to an imaginary line drawn from the tee to your target.

Now, what do you do with the club? Hit the ball, right? But, don't just
toss the ball on the ground and whack at it! You need to place the ball
properly. Using a driver off the tee, you want the ball to be positioned
directly across from the instep of your left heel. Many touring and teaching
professionals advocate moving the ball position by fractions of inches
toward the center of your stance as you progress to the shorter-shafted
(being the higher-numbered) clubs. However, there are also players like
Nancy Lopez and Tom Kite who believe it is better to keep it simple. They
position the ball at the left instep for nearly all shots — perhaps
slightly to the right for short irons because you want these hit with
a descending blow. (Again, specialty shots are another exception.)

You are now ready to swing the club (which follows in Lesson 8). Remember to keep your knees flexed — not bent, but gently relaxed. If you find yourself "topping" the ball (hitting it on top and having it trickle off the tee or go only very short distances), you are probably either hitting with stiff knees or beginning with your knees flexed and then straightening them during your swing.

One final thought: Keep your eyes on the ball! Some instructors have said to "keep your head down," but that is not sound advice according to great golfers like Lopez, Kite, and his mentor, Harvey Penick. Keeping your head down does not allow it to glide slightly back and forth with the rhythm of your swing. It may also keep you from following through properly. It's also harder to pick up the flight of your ball so you can see where it lands.

Many great golfers use "Keep your eyes on the ball" as their "single swing thought." Trying to think about too many things will not help our basic command: RELAX!

That's not a bad command for Christian lives as well. Relax! In his book, *When I Relax, I Feel Guilty*, Tim Hansel gives four commandments for learning to relax in the Lord. #1: Thou shalt live here and now. God is within us, is happening here and now, and the paradox is that we must practice the presence — otherwise it will elude us. #2: Thou shalt not hurry. Hansel says we live too much by the clock — on prearranged timetables and schedules. We must be flexible and willing to sometimes set these aside in order to enjoy the true pleasures of life — like taking an autumn walk with our child. #3: Thou shalt not take thyself too seriously. While a poor self-esteem may be a popular cause for many dysfunctions, we more often think too highly of ourselves. Remain childlike (not the same as childish) and keep a sense of humor! #4: Thou Shalt Be Grateful. Two things should be noted: gratitude is not an option for a Christian, and gratitude is the source of peace.

Solid advice for golf and life: RELAX!

"Give thanks in all circumstances, for this is God's will for you in Christ Jesus" (1 Thess. 5:18).

"Always use a swing thought. Only one. Keep it simple." — Tom Watson

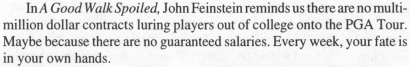

Lesson 9
On Tour with God

In *A Good Walk Spoiled,* John Feinstein reminds us there are no multi-million dollar contracts luring players out of college onto the PGA Tour. Maybe because there are no guaranteed salaries. Every week, your fate is in your own hands.

Life could be worse. While some folks are shoveling snow, players on the PGA, LPGA, and Senior Tours are "working" in Arizona, Hawaii, Puerto Rico, southern California, and other such toasty spots.

The PGA hosts 45 or more official tournaments on their big tour each year; the LPGA over 30 events; and the Senior Tour (for players 50 and over) at least 40 official contests of its own. These tours run from January through October. Then weekly made-for-TV specials in November and December show celebrity tournaments, skins matches, and cross-over events like the J.C. Penney Classic pairing top male and female players.

The ultimate goal of any golf pro is to play the PGA Tour, but players must qualify by passing "Q" school. Beginning with as many as 864 golfers, eliminations are made through three stages until only 180 are left in the final tournament. At the conclusion of this 108-hole event, only the top 40 receive cards for the PGA Tour the following year. The next 70 are given pro cards for the less lucrative Nike Tour that culminates with its own Fall Classic. The top 10 scores from that event also earn exemptions for the regular PGA circuit the following year. Mini-tours like the Ben Hogan Tour and others in the Dakotas, Carolinas, and two in Florida are available for those unsuccessful golfers who want to continue until next year's "Q." There are similar mini-tours overseas as well. (Feinstein followed 17 professionals, including four on the "Q" tour, while researching his book.)

As exciting as even the big tours can be, players are away from home and families a great deal of time. Raymond Floyd combatted that with a practice round with his sons at the 1995 U.S. Open. One of Jack Nicklaus's sons has been "Dad's" caddie on more than one occasion, including his sixth Masters' victory in 1986. When he was out of baseball for a while, Cincinnati Reds manager Ray Knight tried to caddie for wife, Nancy Lopez. They found it was better when he just took care of their young children and watched from the gallery. Mark McCumber even considered leaving the tour life to spend more time with his young son. However, McCumber's older daughters convinced him otherwise. They had enjoyed being able to travel to Disney World and other places around the world to watch their dad play golf, and said it never interfered with his ability to make them feel loved and supported.

Some players have found another support on the PGA Tour. For over 15 years, Larry Moody has conducted a Bible study every Wednesday evening. In 1993 he even baptized a group in a swimming pool at the Walt Disney complex.

Suzanne Strudwick, LPGA 1992 Rookie of the Year, came to the United States from Stratford, England, to "play with the best golfers in the world," but also for such Christian fellowship. "I wasn't getting the support in Europe," says Strudwick. "I attached myself very quickly to the girls in the pro golfers' fellowship." She credits that support

Raymond Floyd
1995 1st year on Senior Tour

(and God's) for helping avoid severe homesickness. "Because I had fellow believers surrounding me . . . I felt very much at home."

Strudwick offers some advice for making such moves: "(1) "Take time to check things out. Listen and observe. Pay attention to others' needs and interests. Don't reject something (or someone) just because they're different. (2) Go with a positive attitude. Don't criticize. Look for the bright side of every situation. (3) Don't change the unchangeable. Don't change convictions just to fit in. Stick to your own goals and life purpose. Keep your commitment to Christ. (4) Have the courage to be yourself. No matter where you are, some people will like you and some won't. Self-control is vital."

Whether it's going on tour or away to college, beginning married life or taking a new job, this is solid advice. Even at home, it's still great advice!

"Be watchful, stand firm in your faith, be courageous, be strong. Let all that you do be done in love" (1 Cor. 16:13;RSV).

"It is the love of family that provides a sense of stability and perspective in Nancy's hectic and demanding world" on the tour. — Don Wade (Foreword for Lopez's book)

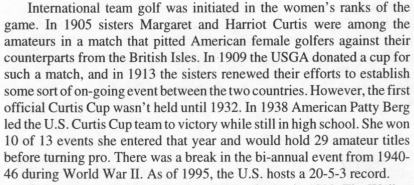

Lesson 10
Team Golf

International team golf was initiated in the women's ranks of the game. In 1905 sisters Margaret and Harriot Curtis were among the amateurs in a match that pitted American female golfers against their counterparts from the British Isles. In 1909 the USGA donated a cup for such a match, and in 1913 the sisters renewed their efforts to establish some sort of on-going event between the two countries. However, the first official Curtis Cup wasn't held until 1932. In 1938 American Patty Berg led the U.S. Curtis Cup team to victory while still in high school. She won 10 of 13 events she entered that year and would hold 29 amateur titles before turning pro. There was a break in the bi-annual event from 1940-46 during World War II. As of 1995, the U.S. hosts a 20-5-3 record.

The equivalent event for male amateurs began in 1922. The Walker Cup was presented by US businessman George Herbert Walker (maternal grandfather of former President George Bush). In 1995 the U.S. also held a commanding lead at 30-3-1. Since 1947 the Walker Cup has been held in odd-numbered years only.

Professionals started their own version of team competition in 1927. British businessman Samuel Ryder donated the Cup for the same trans-Atlantic rivalry. Each team has 12 men, and since 1979 British team eligibility includes all European golfers. The format follows match-play rules and now consists of 5 foursome matches, 5 four-ball matches, and 10 singles matches. A single point is awarded for each match victory. After their 15-13 victory, U.S. Ryder Cup Captain Tom Watson said, "It was my biggest thrill in golf, bigger even than eight major titles." Constantino Rocca, playing for Europe in 1995, recorded an ace — only the third one in Ryder Cup history. The U.S. leads 23-6-2 through 1995. Seven-time Ryder Cup member Tom Kite has been chosen as the 1997 U.S. captain.

Ryder Cup players in the 1993 competition also met as members of the body of Christ. Paul Azinger, Corey Pavin, Jim Gallagher Jr, Chip Beck, and Lee Janzen (all U.S.) and Bernhard Langer (Europe) and their wives attended a Bible study during the week's activities with Larry Moody, PGA Bible teacher. Nearly 350 people attended a Sunday service at the 18th green on the final day of play.

The LPGA began similar match play in 1990 against Europe. The Karsten Manufacturing Company (makers of Ping clubs) donated the Solheim Cup for this event. Both the women and men professionals also play other international team events. LPGA stars play in the Nichirei International; and the PGA in the President's Cup. Both were defending champs in 1996.

Junior amateurs play team golf as well. Following Ryder Cup rules, the American Junior Golf Association (AJGA) Canon Cup is an East-West competition with the best young female and male golfers — ten each selected for the two teams. Senior vice president of Canon, David Farr, says at this event "you meet the future."

Local duffers enjoy team golf as well. Many weekend threesomes or foursomes play either "best ball" or "scramble" competitions. In a best ball, everyone keeps track of their individual strokes but you record only the lowest score on your team per hole. In a scramble, all players drive from the tee. Then the group selects the best shot, and all the teammates shoot their second shot from that spot, and so goes the rest of the round. Some events restrict using the same player's ball on consecutive shots. Both formats are popular for church and business outings or for charity and political fund raising events. Especially in a scramble, even if you are a real hacker you can help the team. You may be a better bunker player that someone else who can drive the ball well. Even a missed putt can show a fellow teammate how to better align his/her putt for a birdie.

This is the same concept with the body of Christ. We each contribute with our own God-given gifts. Some may be hands to perform a service; or feet to keep a project moving along. Others may have the heart of real caregivers; and still others the eyes with a "vision" for future growth. With Jesus as our Head, we are each a vital part of His body — the Church. Just as a person's human body is pronounced dead when the brainwaves flatline, so we must count on Christ if we are to remain alive spiritually and fulfill His mission in the world.

"Now you are the body of Christ, and each one of you is a part of it" (1 Cor. 12:27).

"When Americans apply themselves to winning something as seriously as they have with the Ryder Cup, you have to cope with a very, very ruthless animal." — Bernard Gallacher (1993 European Ryder Cup captain)

Lesson 11
The House that Jack Built

Every golf course has its own atmosphere and no two are alike. Eighteen holes can be tucked in along the shores of an ocean (like Pebble Beach) or built in the midst of the sandy desert (like Starr Pass in Tucson). Lesser-known local courses also have their unique flavor, like the heart-shaped sixth green at Willow Bend in Van Wert, Ohio.

The "Road Hole," 17th at St. Andrews (where the British Open is sometimes held), "is known as the hardest par-4 in the world because it's a par-5," says Ben Crenshaw. Tip Anderson, caddie at St. Andrews for 48 years, agrees with that assessment: "Play it for a 5, and you might just make a 4. Play it like a 4 and get a 7. A hole this old owes you nothing. Respect the hole."

Many of today's leading golfers have become course architects. Muirfield (site of the PGA Memorial) and the Grizzly (near Kings Island where the Senior Kroger is played) are two of several courses Jack Nicklaus has helped design. Arnold Palmer, Greg Norman, and others are also designing courses. Tom Weiskopf, architect for Loch Lomand Golf Club in Scotland, took an early morning walk to take another look at the layout of the 14th hole. Leaping over the stream, he fell into the murky chest-high grass of a peat bog, which acted like quicksand. After literally hours of alternating between relaxation and inch-by-inch tugging on the sharp grass, Weiskopf was able to free himself. For years the hole tended to "spook" him. No wonder!

Alistair Mackenzie, a Scottish doctor who gave up medicine for life as a golf administrator, was among the first to design various courses. His ideas for arranging two loops (a front nine and back nine) for a course and the difficulty for each loop are basically still followed today. He believed each course needed to be "interesting" and arranged so even a high handicapper would enjoy the game (but also be "stimulated to improve"). Considered three of Mackenzie's best designed courses are Cypress Point, Royal Melbourne, and Augusta National.

Writing of Augusta, sports columnist Paul Daughtery says, "On the par-3 16th hole, the sun breaks through the tall loblolly pines at close to noon. From the elevated tee, the hillsides fall away and churn in exploding acres of color. Azaleas erupt like a pastel waterfall, pink and red and white." Don't let beauty fool you. Another par-3 (the 12th) was ranked the eighth toughest hole on the PGA Tour in 1993. Gene Sarazen proved that even on the mighty courses, legends can be made. Back in 1955 he double-eagled the 500-yard par-5 at Augusta.

Fuzzy Zoeller enjoys both the difficulty and beauty of Augusta. In a play-off with Tom Watson and Ed Sneed for the 1979 Masters championship, while Watson thought about golf, Zoeller looked at the world around him and decided it was wonderful. He said, "This is the closest I'll get to heaven."

"I feel God in the trees and grass and flowers, in the rabbits and the birds and the squirrels, in the sky and in the water. I feel at home." shares Harvey Penick. "What a beautiful place a golf course is!" Describing his home course in Texas, he says, "The spring breeze and the rolling greenery with the blue waters of Lake Austin sparkling below . . . it's as good and peaceful a place I know on this earth."

Do you need some peace in your life? Find a spot in the great outdoors and soak in the presence of God, our Creator. Take a friend or go alone. It might be by a cascading brook or near the rhythm of an ocean tide. It might be deep in the shade of your favorite woods or just sitting on your back porch. Who knows? It might even be on a golf course somewhere.

"In his hand are the depths of the earth, and the mountain peaks belong to him. The sea is his, for he made it, and his hands formed the dry land. Come, let us kneel before the Lord our Maker" (Ps. 95: 4-6).

"Golf — where else can you stand out there in acres and acres of glorious lawns you don't have to mow?" — P.J. O'Rourke (guest on the Tom Snyder Show, November 24, 1995)

Lesson 12

Fore!

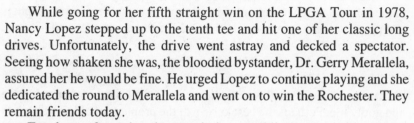

While going for her fifth straight win on the LPGA Tour in 1978, Nancy Lopez stepped up to the tenth tee and hit one of her classic long drives. Unfortunately, the drive went astray and decked a spectator. Seeing how shaken she was, the bloodied bystander, Dr. Gerry Merallela, assured her he would be fine. He urged Lopez to continue playing and she dedicated the round to Merallela and went on to win the Rochester. They remain friends today.

For those of us who play regularly on public courses with average golfers, "Fore" is more commonly heard than on the professional tours. "Fore" is an abbreviation for the word "forewarn" and is yelled to warn you that someone has hit a ball that might be coming your way. Don't turn back or look up when you hear "Fore!" That is a sure way to get smacked in the head. The best way to protect yourself is to put your arms over your face and head and wait a few seconds. Listen for the "thud" of the ball landing nearby rather than looking back toward an oncoming missile.

There are other areas of protection we need to take when playing golf as well. Always wear proper clothing. Don't dress too warmly on hot days. Drink plenty of fluids (water is best) before, after, and while you play to avoid dehydration and heat strokes. Wearing a hat to help shade your eyes and face is also advisable, and remember to wear sun screen to guard against skin cancer. Always take along rain gear in case of a sudden downpour. Do not stay on the course during storms, and never play in lightning. Make certain your golf umbrella is made with a plastic shaft and handle.

"A word to the wise is sufficient" is an old cliché. "Fore!"

God's forewarning to people is called prophecy. The Bible lists 39 names of men and 6 women considered to be annointed by God as prophets and prophetesses. Two books in the Old Testament are referred to as the "major prophets" — Isaiah and Jeremiah. The 15 books from the Lamentations of Ezekiel through Malachi are called the "minor prophets."

These prophets spoke to the people not only of impending doom and destruction, but also with words of how to live a fuller, more productive and godly life. Perhaps the best known of the prophets of old, Isaiah made some of the most significant and meaningful prophecies, especially his foretelling of the birth of Jesus Christ.

President of Dallas Theological Seminary Chuck Swindoll calls it Isaiah's "incredible zenith" when he predicted the birth of the Messiah. "Eight hundred years later(!) . . . the cry from that Infant's throat broke through the centuries of silence." Swindoll writes with both sadness and joy, "Everybody should have believed, but they didn't. Strangely . . . most still don't." Do you believe?

"Therefore, the Lord himself will give you a sign: The virgin will be with child and will give birth to a son, and will call him Immanuel" (Isa. 7:14).

"Whenever I play with him, I usually try to make it a foursome — the President [Ford], myself, a paramedic, and a faith healer."
— Bob Hope

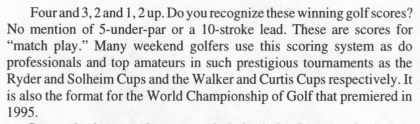

Lesson 13
Fellowship

Four and 3, 2 and 1, 2 up. Do you recognize these winning golf scores? No mention of 5-under-par or a 10-stroke lead. These are scores for "match play." Many weekend golfers use this scoring system as do professionals and top amateurs in such prestigious tournaments as the Ryder and Solheim Cups and the Walker and Curtis Cups respectively. It is also the format for the World Championship of Golf that premiered in 1995.

In match play, you keep score hole by hole. Count each player's strokes and the one with the fewest strokes wins the hole; the player winning the most holes wins the match. Leisure golfers can play out the complete 18 hole course, but in professional competitions, if you are ahead by more than the number of holes remaining to be played, the match is over. Thus the first score in the above paragraph means a player is ahead by 4 with only 3 holes to play. It would be impossible for the opponent to even tie the match at that point.

A variation of match play is Skins, where each hole (or "skin") usually involves a prize, most often money. A tie, called "halving the hole," means the prize carries over to the next hole. Each year four top pros are invited to play in the PGA event held the weekend after Thanksgiving. The first six holes are worth $20,000 each; holes 7 through 12 are worth $30,000 each; and the final six holes, $40,000 each. Playing against Arnold Palmer, Jack Nicklaus, and Tom Watson, Gary Player pulled in $170,000

Fred "Boom Boom" Couples
One of the tour's long hitters

to win the first PGA Skins Game in 1983. Think about the pressure of a five-hole carry-over! Fred Couples collected $270,000 on the fifth play-off hole in 1995 for the "richest hole" in Skins' history, passing the previous record held by Payne Stewart, the only three-consecutive-year winner (1991-92-93) of the event. Jan Stephenson won the first Ladies Skins in 1990 and Dottie Pepper won in 1995. Senior Skins began in 1988 with Chi Chi Rodriguez winning the first two years. In 1995, two-time defending champion Raymond Floyd set a Senior Skins record by winning $420,000. (He three-peated by winning the event in 1996.)

A rather odd format, where the high score wins, is used at the PGA International each year. Called the "Modified Stableford" scoring system, points are awarded after each hole: +8 points for a double-eagle (3 under par); +5 for an eagle (2 under); and +2 for a birdie (one under). You get zero points for a par and -1 for a bogey (one-over-par) and -2 for a double-bogey or worse. Cuts were made after each round and scores reset to 0. The first winner, in 1986, was Ken Green with +12. The best score through 1992 was Joey Sindelar in 1988 with a +17. Starting in 1993, points are totaled for all four rounds. Phil Mickelson won that year with +45; Lee Janzen won in 1995 with +34.

Other popular formats are best ball and scrambles. Most people are more familiar with standard stroke (or medal) play on a par-72 course. Whatever format or scoring system you use, enjoy the game and the fellowship with other golfers.

That should be one of the main goals of church attendance for us. First and foremost, we come to worship Jesus Christ. But church should also be a place of fellowship where we come to really know and appreciate one another. Within the larger church universal, we also need to better appreciate one another and not dwell on our differences. It is time the various denominations quit sniping at one another. This is NOT an appropriate arena in which to play "one up." We need to work together in ecumenical ways to produce far wider reaching efforts than any one church could by itself.

Just as there are many formats in the game of golf, there are many ways to worship God. The formality of the services, the rites that are acknowledged, the various ways to serve communion, etc. — all these are inconsequential in our fellowship and service. Jesus Christ unites us all.

"I appeal to you, in the name of our Lord Jesus Christ, that you all agree . . . so that there may be no divisions among you and that you may be perfectly united in mind and thought" (1 Cor. 1:10).

"It's not like a regular tournament; you don't have to hit the ball great for 18 holes . . . in a Skins game, a putt or two will win for you." — Fred Couples

48

Lesson 14
Sponsors and Charity

One of the most enjoyable parts of many PGA tournaments is the Pro-Am round where celebrities from the entertainment industry, politics, and other sports play with the pros. Many like Jack Lemmon, Mickey Rooney, Yogi Berra, and Kenny Rogers have played these rounds for years. New players join them every week. Hootie and the Blowfish make up their own foursome and practice regularly while on musical tours. Some of the better celebs to watch are TV star John Wagner, country music's Vince Gill, NBA super-star Michael Jordan, and Denver QB John Elway. Some are even considering the PGA Senior Tour when they turn 50. Former Presidents Ford and Bush play regularly. Ford sunk two consecutive 20-foot putts in an early 1996 event. An excellent player, former Vice-President Dan Quayle was a member of the DePauw University golf team while in college.

The celebrities' appearances also help raise money for various charities who receive proceeds from the PGA tournaments. Bing Crosby, Bob Hope, and Danny Thomas, along with Dinah Shore on the LPGA, were among the first to host events to raise such funds. Many entertainers and athletes sponsor local charity golf events in the cities where they play and live that also benefit worthy organizations. For years Boomer Esaison sponsored such an event in Cincinnati to raise money for juvenile diabetes. He now works with similar events for cystic fibrosis.

Corporate sponsorship has contributed to the success of not just enlarged prize money on the tours but has greatly increased giving to charity. Nearly every event has a sponsor who pays up to $1.7 million for that privileged way of advertising. In addition, there are the commercial ads that run during the TV events that add money to the charity coffers. Buick sponsors two such tournaments a year. Coca Cola, IBM, Merrill Lynch, NEC, and Motorola are but a few others on the PGA Tour. On the ladies tour Chick-Fil-A, Sara Lee, Oldsmobile, Corning, and others invest money. JC Penney sponsors a combined event near the conclusion of the season that pairs PGA and LPGA players.

Charity is the leading money-winner of the Senior Tour. While the running joke is that "you never say stroke to an old person," the Senior Tour is proud of their partnership with Bayer Aspirin in their efforts for "Strokes Against Strokes." During the month of May, Team Bayer contributes $500 per birdie to the Heart Association. They also promote that individuals take an aspirin-a-day for stroke prevention.

Senior golfer Dave Stockton said one of the biggest moments for him personally was being chairman of the Relief Efforts for Oklahoma where the PGA raised almost half a million dollars to build a new day care center for the kids after the bombing of the federal building devastated the area and lives in 1995.

Total PGA tournaments eclipsed the $300 million mark in 1995.

Many pros donate personal time for similar causes. Jim Gallagher put together a package with Delta Airlines, Inside the PGA, and Walt Disney to arrange a special visit to the Disney complex for a nine-year-old leukemia patient in his home town. Gallagher and his family made the trip with the Gilmer family, and Jim said it was little Lindsey that gave him the inspiration to win the 1995 Fed Ed St. Jude Tournament. "God has a way of putting things in order," said Gallagher.

Individual giving from golfers is not new. Patty Berg, champion in the 1950s, donated time and money to charities throughout her career. She said her father taught her early, "If you're going to play the game, you're going to do some charity work for people."

What or who inspires you? Whom do you inspire with your efforts and financial support for worthwhile organizations? How much do you commit to the Missions programs at your church? God instructs us we are to tithe (give 10 percent of our income) to His church — that's off the top. Sacrificial giving goes well beyond that. If every person, even every Christian who attends worship services regularly, would give this 10 percent, we might be able to eliminate welfare and other poverty programs in our nation and around the world. Only when we give sacrificially can God's "will on earth be done."

"Each of you must bring a gift in proportion to the way the Lord your God has blessed you" (Deut. 16:17).

"I didn't invent corporate involvement in golf. I just recognized the potential it had to help build the game." — Deane Beman (PGA Commissioner)

Lesson 15
Seasoned Golfers

"Golf is the only game I know where as you get to senior status, you can make adjustments that enable you to keep up with the youngsters." So says Gary Player, now a regular on the PGA Senior Tour. The handicap system is one way to make the adjustment. Another is by club selection and strategy as you get older.

"Pace off the carry you get with every club," says Player, and "play your shot, not someone else's" (not even your own from years gone by). Player advises replacing your 1, 2, 3 irons with 5 and 7 woods and suggests that if you have trouble getting the ball up in the air, try metal woods and sole-weighted irons. Harvey Penick suggests using clubs with more flexible shafts and composition grips that are more flexible.

You may need to adjust your swing to protect back muscles, and *always* **warm** up before you play. Flexibility and stretching exercises are a must! Place your club behind your back and twist side-to-side before each round — and while you wait your turn on other tees. Also, remember to drink plenty of water and dress appropriately.

Penick loved golf because it was "a game you can play all your life." He believed "seasoned citizens" learned to enjoy the game even more — to "value freedom, companionship, being outdoors, beautiful surroundings, and the game itself." The older we get, the more we understand that golf (like all sports) is "only a game."

Senior PGA players seem to understand this. Watch how they

truly enjoy the game and one another. Dave Stockton, says, "When the first Senior Tour started, it was like a showcase for the Sam Sneads and a second chance for fans to see them. Now it's become more competitive — and we're having fun." Many names on the leader boards are new to golf fans. Former doctors, a tire salesman, club pros, coaches, and others who never made the PGA Tour have found their way to the senior circuit. When former Naval Academy golf coach Larry Ringer played in the Senior Open, he found, "The only thing better than playing with Arnold Palmer is playing better than Arnold Palmer." Ringer shot a 68 in the first round, while Arnie had a 72. Imagine how much fun that was!

One of the names often found on the Senior leader board is Jim Colbert. When asked what his best tournament or round of golf has been he said he "hoped it hasn't happened yet." He still wants to improve and thrives on the competition, but he also talks about how much fun it is playing with the likes of Lee Trevino. Colbert kids Trevino in an interview where Lee said, "I can hardly wait to get up each day — to go grab my clubs and to see what I'm going to say that day." Trevino also said, "One nice thing about the Senior Tour is that you can take a cart and a cooler. If your game is not going well, you can always have a picnic."

Another gallery favorite, Chi Chi Rodriguez, does the famous sword dance with his putter once he hits the cup. One of his best lines about aging: "The older you are, the longer you used to be." Add a Bob Bruce one-liner: "What's nice about our tour is you can't remember your bad shots." Even Palmer gets in a quip now and then: "You know you're getting old when all the names in your little black book have M.D. after them."

"Nobody grows old merely by living a number of years," said General Douglas MacArthur. Rev. Robert Strand repeats the general's philosophy: "People grow old by deserting their ideals. Years may wrinkle the skin, but to give up interest wrinkles the soul." In *Moments with Grandparents,* Strand shares from former British prime minister Benjamin Disraeli, "If people are rightly aging, they are growing in wisdom, and as their years increase so does this wisdom."

Chuck Swindoll concurs. "Aging isn't a choice. But our response to it is. In so many ways, we determine ourselves how we shall grow old." In his book, *Strengthening Your Grip* (great golf title!), Swindoll says, "Because we cannot alter the inevitable, we adjust to it." He suggests two responses or adjustments for aging. First, "view life as a challenge not a threat" and then "follow the Lord fully, not half-heartedly."

"Gray hair is a crown of splendor; it is attained by a righteous life" (Prov. 16:31). (Getting gray? Just tell people you are getting more righteous!)

"I went to bed and I was old and washed up. I woke up a rookie. What could be better!" — Raymond Floyd (on turning 50 and joining the Senior Tour)

Lesson 16

Champions

Both tennis and golf have four major Grand Slam tournaments each year. However, as sports author John Feinstein points out, "While you may be in a field of 128, winning each event in tennis, you only have to beat seven players. To win a golf tournament, you have to beat the entire field."

The only golfer to ever win all four Grand Slam events in a single year was Bobby Jones in 1920, when the Big Four were the U.S. and British Open and U.S. and British Amateurs. Jones won the U.S. Open four times; the Brit Open three times; and the U.S. Amateur five times. He also founded the Masters Tournament in 1934.

Beginning in 1960, golf's Grand Slam consisted of the Masters, the PGA Championship, and the U.S. and British Opens. No golfer has won all four in one year. Ben Hogan had three of the wins in 1953 and several have garnered two legs of the prize in a single year, including Jack Nicklaus five times and Arnold Palmer and Tom Watson, twice. Hogan, Nicklaus, Gary Player, and Gene Sarazen have each won all four events but not in a single year. On the LPGA side, the four tournaments to win (since 1983) are the: U.S. Open, du Maurier Classic (in Canada), Dinah Shore Nabisco, and LPGA Championship. Babe Zaharias (1950), Mickey Wright (1961), and Pat Bradley (1986) have each won three events in a season but no one has ever made the Grand Slam.

A made-for-TV special, the Grand Slam Tournament invites the respective winner of each GS event. For 1995 that included: U.S. Open, Corey Pavin; Brit Open, John Daly; PGA, Steve Elkington; and Masters, Ben Crenshaw. The inauguration of the World Championship of Golf that used Sony rankings to schedule four worldwide regional play-offs throughout the year was in 1995. The four area winners were Mashiro Kuramoto (Japanese Tour); Mark McCumber (U.S./PGA); Barry Lane (Europe); and David Frost (remainder of the world). Lane won the match-play event.

We can look at other interesting statistics for champions. Player-of-the-Year awards have gone to Tom Watson (6 times), Jack Nicklaus (4), Ben Hogan (3), and on the LPGA, Kathy Whitworth (7 times). There are awards for the lowest scoring average each year. Named for Glenna Collett Vare (6-time U.S. Amateur winner) and Harry Varden (6-time British Open champ), respective winners have been: Kathy Whitworth (7 times), JoAnne Carner and Mickey Wright (5), Patty Berg, Nancy Lopez, and Judy Rankin (3); Billy Casper and Lee Trevino (5 times), Arnold Palmer and Sam Snead (4), Ben Hogan and Tom Watson (3).

Byron Nelson set a record most believe will never be equaled — with 11 victories in a row (18 altogether) in 1945. He averaged 68.33 that year and won 45 percent (34 of 75) of the events he entered during the 1944-45-46 seasons. Nelson played 113 events without missing the cut for the final round. The first pro golfer to turn commentator (and to have a tour event named after him — the GTE Byron Nelson Classic), he is the volunteer starter at the Masters each year.

The World Golf Hall of Fame, now located with the International Golf Museum in St. Johns County, Florida, initiated its first members in 1974. Included were Berg, Walter Hagen, Hogan, Jones, Nelson, Nicklaus, Francis Ouimet, Palmer, Player, Sarazen, Snead, Vardon, and Zaharias.

How do we become champions in life? Do we need some Hall of Fame for recognition before we feel we have been successful?

Sports figure in NBA management through the years Pat Williams says to notice how we greet people. We usually begin conversations with, "What do you do?' Seldom do we ask, "How are you as a parent?" or "What kind of husband are you?" He does not mean to lessen the importance of our jobs (and our dedication to them), but Williams believes the highest sign of success, "the highest compliment that can be paid" to anyone is to be "Christlike."

It is not our "doing" that makes us a success. It is our "being" and the best thing we can be is like Christ.

"Commit to the Lord whatever you do, and your plans will succeed" (Prov. 16:3).

"No matter where I finish — first, second, third, or last — doesn't change my standing with the Lord. He's more concerned with the golfer than the tournament." — Tom Lehman

Lesson 17
What's Your Handicap?

Golf is one of the few sports that makes adjustments to scores so regular duffers can compete with more advanced players. If you plan to enter many local tournaments or want to qualify for the U.S. Amateur Open, you can check at your local golf club to find out how to certify an official handicap using the rather complex USGA Index.

For those of us who are weekend players or novices, there are easier ways to compute a handicap so we feel competitive on the course with better golfers.

The "Second Best" system uses your three best scores on a regulation course (par-68 or more). Using your second best score, subtract 70 for men and 73 for women. Subtract that number of strokes from your completed round of play. Until you have played three rounds, you may subtract 74 (men) or 77 (women). The maximum number of HC strokes: 36 for men and 40 for women.

With the Peoria Handicap System, you pre-select a par-3 hole, a par-5 hole, and four par-4 holes (representative of all par-4's in length and difficulty). When the round is complete, add your strokes *over* par on these six holes. This is the HC to be deducted from your raw score. (There is a maximum of three over on the par-3 and par-4 holes and four over on the par-5.)

Two somewhat more complicated HC formulas are often used for beginners. Both the Callaway and Scheid Systems use the "worst hole" scores on holes 1 through 16 only. There is a sliding scale of how many worst holes may be subtracted at the end of the round. Anyone shooting 72 or below gets no handicap. Scores with 73-75 get to subtract half of their "worst hole." 76-80 get the full amount of their worst; 86-90 gets two worst holes, and so on all the way up to a gross score of 126 which gets six worst holes. (You cannot use more than twice the par for any worst hole score. For instance, even if you shoot 12 on a par-5, you can only subtract 10.) Peoria's sliding scale goes to 126 and has a maximum HC of 50, whereas the Scheid goes up to 151 and has no max.

Another easy way to handicap beginners (until they can establish their own HC) is to allow 50 strokes per round by giving them 3 strokes per hole, except on par-3 holes.

Handicaps off the golf course take on a different meaning. Many people have overcome supposed handicaps to succeed in life. Fanny Crosby (famed writer of many of our favorite hymns) was blind, but her mother encouraged her to climb trees and act as much like normal children as possible. Tom Sullivan, blind actor, author, and musician, believes everyone has a handicap of some sort. It might be shyness or talking too much or being too aggressive. It might be growing up in a dysfunctional family or a severe illness. Sullivan learned to make the most of his handicap. He says to "concentrate on what you have, not what you don't have." He plays regulation golf and challenges others to a round letting them choose the course if he can call the tee-time. He gets an advantage by playing at night.

Some would say Paul Azinger lost his advantage after winning the

Paul Azinger
On his way back after cancer

Toledo Open in 1994. Seeing a doctor for soreness in his shoulder, Zinger found out he had cancer. He underwent surgery and a full round of chemotherapy. Who would have thought he would be able to return for any of the 1995 Tour? Through his determination to overcome the nasty side effects of the illness and his faith in Jesus, Azinger returned (bald head and all) to defend his title in Toledo in 1995.

What do you need to overcome in your life? What handicap is teaching you lessons? How can you let God use it to make you a better person?

"You, dear children, are from God and have overcome them, because the one who is in you is greater than the one who is in the world" (1 John 4:4).

"It's not important what we accomplish in life, but what we overcome." — Johnny Miller (advice to Azinger during his bout with cancer)

Lesson 18
Courtesy and Honesty

At the NEC World Series of Golf in 1995, Greg Norman refused to sign the scorecard of Mark McCumber. Norman insisted that McCumber had removed a spiked-up blade of grass in his line of putt on the seventh green. That would have been illegal. McCumber said it was a bug whose removal was acceptable. The commissioner of the tournament said he took both men at their word, but Norman threatened to withdraw and leave when McCumber was not penalized. Such contested plays happen more often than you might think. Similar accusations have been made by Tom Watson against Gary Player, Hale Irwin against Seve Ballesteros, and Seve against Paul Azinger.

Golf has an honor code perhaps above most other sports. Interpreting the rules of play may be all in our perspective, but honesty should be unquestionable. Following the rules and proper etiquette on the course helps everyone enjoy the game more. It is largely a matter of common sense and respect for others.

When in the teeing area, don't talk loudly, move around, or do anything that might distract the golfer preparing to drive. Always let the person who had the lowest score on the previous hole have the "honor" of driving first.

Make certain players in front of your group are safely out of the way before you drive. Should you hit the ball further than expected and it heads for anyone, immediately yell "Fore!" as loudly as you can. Help "spot" the ball for all the other players in your group and yell the warning for them as they may not see where the errant shot is headed as quickly as you can.

Don't loiter. Play without delay as much as possible. If anyone in your group loses a ball, help look for it. Signal for groups behind you to "play through" (ahead of you) while you search.

Before leaving a bunker, make certain you fill in and smooth over any footprints you have made. (A rake should be nearby or in the sand trap to assist with this repair.) Also replace any large divots you may leave in the fairways. Place the tuft of grass back in the hole and tamp in place with your foot. Once on the green, make any repairs to turf damage you may cause there as well. (A tee or special turf tool is useful for this purpose.)

Never drop the flagstick, clubs, or your bag on the green. Place the pin gently on the putting surface out of the line of play for any of the golfers in your group. Never walk between another player's ball and the cup, as you may cause an indentation or other problem in the pathway of his ball. The person whose ball is furthest from the hole putts first.

It is best to place your bags off of the green in the direction of the next tee. As soon as everyone has finished putting, move off the green immediately so the next group can make their approach shots. (You can mark your scores on the way to, or at, the next tee.)

Have respect for everyone in your group and others on the course. Having respect for everyone around us in our daily lives is good advice as well. Honesty and respect go hand in hand.

"People who cheat lack self-respect," says Michael Goldman, professor of philosophy at Miami University. Dealing with students who use term papers written by someone else (usually from a fraternity/sorority file), copy answers on exams, and find other creative ways to cheat, he has learned, "They are insecure about their own ability to succeed and too cowardly to accept occasional failure." He is concerned that "cheaters have not mastered the knowledge, skills, etc. required in their jobs." But most of all Goldman is concerned about character. "What kind of person cheats?" he asks. If students go unpunished, he fears this "encourages laziness, dishonesty in other matters, and a lack of integrity that will be reflected in all dimensions of a person's life."

Teaching our children to be kind, courteous, and honest in all matters should be among our top priorities. Setting a good example in these areas is still the best way to teach.

"Whatever happens, conduct yourselves in a manner worthy of the gospel of Christ" (Phil. 1:27).

"Fine manner and good taste are at the heart of the game. To cheat in golf is to cheat against yourself." — Malcolm Campbell (Random House International Encyclopedia of Golf)

Lesson 19
Leading Money-Winners

After three years on the mini-tours, Tom Lehman's total earnings averaged out to $13,000 a year, a mere pittance compared to expenses. Without sponsorship, he could not have survived. In 1989 Lehman was down to his final $500 to stay on tour. Going overseas was his "last effort." Finishing second in the South African Open and winning $30,000 kept him alive for two more years until his being named Player-of-the-Year on the Hogan Tour landed him on the PGA Tour.

Corey Pavin has fond memories of South Africa as well, but his $1 million purse at the Gary Player course in December 1995 was a bit more lucrative. Also in 1995, the Inaugural Andersen Consulting World Championship of Golf winner, Barry Lane of Europe, took home $1 million. These special events are not recorded as a part of the regular PGA Tour money list.

Arnold Palmer was the first to go over the $1 million mark in total earnings on the PGA Tour. The award for the leading money-winner each year is now presented in his name. Greg Norman won the award in 1995 setting a single-season record with $1.6 million. He won 3 of 16 events and averaged over $100,000 per tourney. Named PGA Player-of-the-Year in 1995, Norman became the all-time leading money-winner with over 9.5 million dollars, surpassing Tom Kite.

Curtis Strange was the first to earn $1 million in a single year in Tour events back in 1988. The most money won in a single season without a victory was by Payne Stewart in 1993 earning $982,875. Billy Mayfair, who finished second to Norman in earnings in 1995, speaks for most players on Tour. It isn't the money that counts the most. "What drives me is the competition," says Mayfair.

Golf phenom at Stanford University, Tiger Woods, is not driven by money either. At 18, he was the youngest winner of the U.S. Amateur Open in 1993 and repeated in 1994. He was also the first to win three U.S. Junior Championships, and the youngest to play in the LA Open at age 16. With his talent and personality, Woods is a money bonanza waiting to explode with lucrative endorsements at his beck and call, but he's not ringing up sponsors yet. He intends to complete all four years of college. His mom, Kutilda, says, "We're not parents who are out for the money. I always tell Tiger that golf is not a priority. Nobody can take an education away from you. Spend four years at Stanford and improve yourself."

Perhaps that's a woman's perspective. While balancing home life and the Tour a bit more tightly than their male counterparts, LPGA players have also found the prize money has not been as lucrative until recently. Now a fairway commentator for ESPN, Judy Rankin was the first female golfer to win over $100,000 in a year back in 1976. Betsy King became the all-time leading money-winner in LPGA history in 1995. Rolex Player-of-the-Year in 1984, 1989, and 1993, King finally won her 30th tournament on the LPGA Tour in 1995 which puts her in the Hall of Fame.

However, it's not fame or money that matters most to King. Her perspective comes from a Bible study lesson. King shared with freelance writer Mike Sandrolini: "It's not, 'What am I gonna do for God?' but 'God, what do You want me to do? Where are You working and how can I help?' " She enjoys helping with Habitat for Humanity and encouraged the LPGA Christian Fellowship to become involved as well. Barb Thomas, whose first tour victory was at the Hawaiian Open in 1995, was also among the group that toured orphanages as a part of "Romanian Relief." King won golf's Charles Bartlett Award in 1993 for "unselfish contributions to the betterment of society."

"We've made a difference, I think," says King. "Obviously you don't change the world, but you try to change the world you're in."

What does Missions mean in your life? Where and how in your world is God asking you to help?

"Riches do not endure forever, and a crown is not secure for all generations" (Prov. 27:24).

"In terms of material things, they have very little, but spiritually, they're so much more rich than we are. They truly have to rely on the Lord." — Barb Thomas (speaking of the Romanians she met on the LPGA Mission Trip)

Lesson 20

Which Club Should I Use?

Before buying any expensive golf clubs, be sure you feel comfortable with them. Borrow clubs from friends or practice on the range outside the pro shop. Make certain they feel right and are properly weighted for you. Women and junior golfers especially tend to use clubs that are too heavy and too long.

Harvey Penick believed the average player could score better with a 3-wood off the tee than with a driver. See which works best for you. Why invest in a driver if you aren't going to use it? "You're only giving up perhaps one good drive per round." Many can also use a 3-wood in place of longer (lower-numbered) irons. Kathy Whitworth used a 4- or 5-wood to get out of long grass in the rough — the small head gets under the ball well and the bulk of the wood slides through the thicker grass. Likewise, PGA player Brad Bryant uses a 7-wood from a deep lie in the rough. "It gets you up and out," he says. "The ball should fly high and land softly on the green." Check the shaft on woods or drivers. A stiffer shaft will provide more accuracy (hit straighter), but a softer shaft (like the new "bubble shaft") can be whipped for better distance. Decide which is better for you.

Nancy Lopez says clubs with a slightly rounded sole (the part that rests on the ground when you address the ball) are more "forgiving" when you mis-hit. Also clubs with the heads offset from the shaft help keep your hands naturally ahead of the ball on your swing.

Remember the lower-numbered clubs (both irons and woods) have less trajectory and more distance; higher-numbered clubs more loft and less distance. Since most golfers mis-hit on the short end of distance rather than over-shooting their target, if you can't decide between two clubs, choose the longer club. Tom Watson also says to use more club when the air is damp, shooting into a strong headwind, or shooting at a raised green.

Don't look at distance charts or use the same club as a friend. You must determine your own distance per club. Hours of practice at the driving range will help you judge how far you can hit with each club. Check your own stride so when you pace off distances you will be as accurate as possible.

Specialty clubs improve scores for most golfers. A sand wedge is a designed to glide through the sand and under the ball — throwing out sand with the ball. Use it for shots other than out of a bunker when you have a short approach that requires some bounce. There are also specialty wedges for short shots that don't need bounce. If you aren't accurate in hitting the greens, these specialty clubs would be a wise investment.

The putter is the most personal club in your bag. There are hundreds of models and designs. Experiment until you find the one that gives you the best touch. You must have confidence in your putter. It is the one club you will most likely use on every hole.

Like our putter, the Bible is something we should use regularly. Likewise, the Bible comes in many "models" or translations. A paraphrase has been re-written from other Bibles; a translation returns to the original manuscripts of Hebrew and Greek and then modernizes phraseology and understanding. As with your putter, it is a personal choice. Pray that the Holy Spirit will lead you in whichever version you read.

Just as we carry a variety of clubs, so too, we need to read a variety of materials. Newspapers and current event magazines keep us abreast of what's going on in our community and the world. How can we reach out to help if we don't know what's going on?

Biographies of Christians and other moral leaders show how God has worked in their lives. Christian fiction has become popular as well with series like the "Joshua" books by Joseph Girzone. To remind ourselves that the birth of Jesus was not just a Christmas story, read *Two from Galilee* during Advent each year. Helpful non-fiction is also available for nearly any problem. Ask your pastor, a good friend, or the clerk at a Christian bookstore for suggestions.

Practicing our putting will improve our game perhaps faster than anything. Reading good materials and especially God's Word will improve our lives.

"So it is with my word that goes out from my mouth: It will not return to me empty, but will accomplish what I desire and achieve the purpose for which I sent it" (Isa. 55:11).

"One study says unless you can swing a club at least 85 miles per hour, the 3-wood actually carries farther than the driver." — Chuck Cook (Payne Stewart's coach)

70

Lesson 21

Beach Shots – Sand Trapped

Sand traps in the United States are like "going to the beach for the day" compared to the "old course" of St. Andrews in Scotland. Those bona fide bunkers are deep enough for protective cover in wartime.

The average golfer may fear the sand, but most pros can hit from these as well as from the high grass off the fringe of the green. The secret is (as always) lots of practice. JoAnne Carner once joked, "I stayed in the bunker until I made one. They had to bring me cocktails and dinner."

Byron Nelson, one of the all-time great long bunker players, offers his advice: Work your feet into the sand for balance. Focus on using your legs. Too much "arms" causes you to raise up. Keep knees flexed. Don't "help the ball" into the air. Hit a full, free swing and let the sand take it out. Another clue for fairway bunkers: use one more club-length than usual from that distance.

For greenside bunkers, most of the same advice applies. Your swing will not be as full and there is almost no follow-through at all, especially if your ball is plugged into the sand (called a "fried egg"). Tom Kite suggests "spanking the sand behind the ball." Do not slam your club into the sand, but try to lightly brush it through the length of the shot. Nelson reminds us, "It's the sand that throws the ball out, not the clubhead."

Playing out of the sand requires more wrist action than most shots, especially if your ball is "trapped" at the side of the bunker. To get the feel for this cocked-wrist motion, Nick Faldo suggests practicing with your right hand only on the club. "Feel your right wrist. Retain that feeling as you play the shot."

Another problem with these banked sand shots is the uneven stance you often have. The same basic advice for uneven lies is true anywhere on the course. You want to get your hips as even as possible. On an uphill lie, shorten (or flex) your uphill (left) leg and straighten the (right) leg that is lower. On a downhill lie, your lower leg (left in this case) will be straighter and your uphill (right) leg will be flexed. Gary Player advises when the ball is above your feet, choke down on the club and keep your weight on the balls of your feet; when the ball is below your feet, hold the club at the end and put your weight on the heels. Another suggestion is to use one club more on uphill lies and one club less on downhill lies. One of the main objects in golf and especially the specialty shots is good balance.

The pathway in life is often uneven and if we lose our balance, we feel trapped. Greg Norman went through such a crisis period back in the early nineties. He felt he had sunk to the "bottom of a pit" and admits those were the "worst 27 months of playing the game of golf." But he goes on to say, "That's when you ask yourself a lot of questions and when you learn so much about yourself." He understands the importance of that time of searching. "I became a better person," shares Norman, "not only a better person for myself and my wife and kids but a better person to life in general."

As Christians, we should adopt this same attitude when crises occur. Christian author and family counselor H. Norman Wright says, "Crisis and major life transitions are the stuff life is made of. Crises have the potential for developing Christian character." We need to

Greg Norman
1995 Leading Money Winner

look at crises as opportunities — as chances to "turn for the better." Wright also reminds us that how we see God and whether or not we permit Him to control our lives will make a difference in our reactions to a crisis.

The lesson of the well-known poem "Footprints" is that during the most difficult times we tend to feel God has abandoned us. Even though there is only one set of footprints, we finally come to recognize His presence with us because He is indeed carrying us.

Think of God's presence with you the next time you see footprints in the sand trap of golf or life.

"Free me from the trap that is set before me, for you are my refuge" (Ps. 31:4).

"I really thank that down period in my life for making these future times better off." — Greg Norman

Lesson 22
Practice Anytime

"The harder I practice, the luckier I get," says Gary Player. "Sports author John Feinstein found that golfers are the only athletes who practice *after* the game is over. Nancy Lopez agrees that is definitely the best time to practice. "It helps extend your endurance," she says, "and you can correct what went wrong."

The average hacker heads straight to the clubhouse, grabs some refreshments, commiserates with his friends, and heads for home. When we do return to the practice range for the next round, we tend to work on our strengths, because we like to feel good about ourselves and look good in front of others. We would do better to practice areas of weakness immediately following our game.

This doesn't mean to omit practice time before our next outing. Another common mistake of average golfers is that they spend too much time with their driver at the practice range. Start with the short irons. Spend more time working with those (and chipping and putting). Improving your short game will lower your scores much faster than practicing with your driver. Go to the driver for only the last 4-5 balls left in your practice bucket. Jack Nicklaus also suggests that you "don't change clubs and locations too quickly in practice. Practice with a specific club until the repetition equals consistency."

A couple of helpful practice drills are used by master teachers Harvey Penick and Bob Mann. Penick suggests a slow motion drill. Practice your back swing very, VERY slowly!! As you reach the top of your backswing, come to a stop (check to see if the club is parallel with the ground), re-plant your left foot to begin the downswing — again, very slowly. Stop 1/3 the way down and hold it. See how your muscles feel. Where is your weight centered? Practice this four times in a row and then make your full tempo swing. Repeat this slow motion drill several times a day. Mann suggests using your left hand only on a few practice swings each day. This will establish a good left-hand grip and exercise the muscles in your left arm. It will also make the club seem lighter once you use both hands — which should add to your distance. Even while in the backyard, use a dandelion head or a blade of grass as your ball to practice keeping your clubface in the square position at impact.

On his tape series, Al Geiberger has relaxing, even-tempo music playing in the background as you watch his repetitions of a perfect swing. If you can think of a favorite tune whose rhythm matches your swing, you might be able to hum (even silently) this tune to maintain your tempo. Try it during practice and see if it works for you.

Play games by yourself or with friends when you practice. See if you can hit a shot under a park bench or the branches of a specific tree. See who can hit the ball the highest with a 5 iron or who can get closest to the bunker without going in. Play "Can you make this?" (like the game of HORSE in basketball).

Practice every day in some way. Go to a driving range. Buy a putting cup for indoor practice. Keep an old hula hoop and an old club in the trunk of your car. While you wait for the kids at soccer practice, see how many shots in a row you can chip inside the ring. To improve your game you need the consistency of daily practice.

The same is true in our Christian lives. If we want consistency, we must meet with the Lord daily. Spend time in silence so you can hear His voice. Prayer and devotion time are essential. So are Bible study and regular church attendance. In his book, *The Practice of the Presence of God*, Brother Lawrence believes we can practice God's presence in ALL we say and do. (He did it while scrubbing floors.) He says it takes no theological training nor any special time nor talent. Anywhere, anytime, regardless of what we are doing, we can "practice His presence."

"Blessed are those who have learned to acclaim you, and walk in the light of your presence, O Lord" (Ps. 89:15).

"Ninety-nine point nine percent of the golfers on the PGA Tour can't sleep at night if they don't hit balls after a round." — John Feinstein

Lesson 23
Role Models

The Inaugural Rolex Challenge in 1995 brought together four top amateurs from the AJGA (America Junior Golf Association) and four top players from the PGA and LPGA ranks.

The winner of the 1993 U.S. Open, Laurie Merten, was paired with young Gracie Park who had 22 junior titles and won the 1994 Heather Farr Award as Junior Player of the Year. (Farr was a dynamic young star on the LPGA whose life was cut short after a bout with cancer.) The other female pair for the match play were 15-year-old Beth Bauer with 12 titles in only her second year of tournaments and LPGA player Michelle McGann.

McGann was excited to be able to "give something back" to the AJGA. She had been a Florida state junior champ in her youth and was the 1987 Junior Player of the Year. She thinks it's great experience for these juniors to play alongside the pros. "They can see we make mistakes, too," said McGann, plus "it gives them something to work for."

Like McGann, Phil Mickelson was the 1987 Junior Player of the Year (the first of three consecutive titles). He was paired with Mark Northey, a freshman at Georgia. Both left-handed players, Northey hailed Mickelson as his golf idol and was able to take advantage of many golfing instructors' advice to watch the pros swing as a way of learning. The final pairing for the event was former chairman of the AJGA Davis Love III and 18-year-old Joel Kribel out of Stanford.

All the golfers expressed their appreciation to the AJGA and to

all of those who went before them in the game of golf.
However, in an interview Mickelson shared that his real role
models were his parents. His dad was the biggest influence in his life
—building a putting green and chipping area in their backyard. Mickelson
is right-handed in everything but golf. He said he watched his father play
and "mirrored" his images, thus learning to play as a southpaw.

Many of us look to our parents as our true role models. Some,
however, may have come from dysfunctional homes that were not very
loving. Perhaps you found your role model in an older sister or brother.
Maybe there was a special teacher, coach, scout leader, or minister.

Local pastor Jim Dunaway reminds us that our real role model is
Christ. "With Jesus as our role model of God's unconditional love, we
must attempt to manifest the same spirit as did Christ," says Dunaway.
"Christ lived out His commitment to servanthood. He promoted acceptance, forgiveness, redemption, and restoration." Regardless of our age,
our position of profession, we need these qualities in order to be a role
model for others around us.

*"Don't let anyone look down on you because you are young, but set an
example for the believers in speech, in life, in love, in faith and in purity"*
(1 Tim. 4:12).

"It's great to be a PGA member, believe me . . . but the greatest thing of
all in life is to be called a child of God." — Paul Azinger

Lesson 24
The Clubhouse

When the round of golf is over, the comfort of the clubhouse is like a "Welcome Home" — offering a variety of refreshments to satisfy one's hunger and thirst. Laughter, griping, self-berating, and flattery are all a part of the chatter overheard at the "19th Hole" as golfers relax and talk over their successes and failures.

Many country club lounges are extravagant — like walking into a five-star restaurant or hotel lobby. In smaller rural country clubs or in public course clubhouses the amenities may be somewhat less luxurious, but the time friends spend there before and after golf still brings a closeness and kindred spirit.

Being of "kindred" spirit or related in some like-minded and spiritual way is certainly a part of our family and home life. We share common interests, mutual goals, and dreams for the future. Our home is where we live and relate to one another in a myriad of ways. The structure of the house itself doesn't have much to do with it. While it might be more fun to have a big screen television for the Super Bowl and other special events, it's *who* we share the events with not *what* things are available in the sharing that really matters.

Peggy Benson says, "Home has a good deal more to do with your heart than with your house." In her book, *Listening For a God Who Whispers*, Peggy shares about the many homes she helped create — from a garage to a trailer to a walk-up to a lovely large home by the

Bobby Jones, Ben Hogan
Jimmy Damaret, Byron Nelson

lake. Now a widow with grown children, Peggy has a small townhouse for just her — just her and Jesus. She is learning what Jesus meant when He shared with His disciples at the Last Supper: "I will make my home in you."

Just as we make a place to "recover from the hustle and bustle of the world and its wounds," writes Peggy, "we can make a place for the Lord." She quietly encourages us, "If we can make a place where memories can be found . . . where the special moments of our lives are visited again . . . then we can make a place where the Lord can remind us of the ways His grace found us." And rather poignantly, she says, "If we can live our lives in a way that we can hardly bear to be apart from the things that remind us of home and the life and love that is there, if we can't go away without taking some of it with us . . . then we know something of what it means to be homesick for the Lord."

We need to make homes for our families where we can recover from the pains of everyday living, where we share most precious memories, and where we always feel loved. Most of all we need to make our homes where we meet Jesus and "let Him come in" so that we never feel homesick or apart from Him.

"Unless the Lord builds the house, its builders labor in vain" (Ps. 127:1).

"Folks always painted me like something out of 'Li'l Abner'; but I'm proud of where I was born, and proud of the folks I came from." — Sam Snead

Lesson 25
Get Close

On the 18th hole at Kaui, Hawaii, Ben Crenshaw pitched a short shot that took one bounce and went into the cup to win the 1995 Grand Slam Tournament. Most average golfers stand in awe of such short game mastery.

"Getting up and down" — which means pitching or chipping shots just short of the green (getting up) and sinking the putt (down) in the hole — is the "most important key to improving your game," according to Al Geiberger.

What is the difference between pitching and chipping? A pitch has a high arc that lands softly near the pin, often with backspin. A chip is more of a low running shot that hits the green and then rolls to the cup. Because the clubface of your irons become more lofted with the shorter (higher-numbered) clubs, you would use a 9 iron for a pitch and more likely a 7 or 8 iron for a chip. If your game includes a lot of pitch and chip shots, you might want to consider buying specialty wedges.

You want to pitch the ball if you have a good lie, an uphill lie, a soft green (where the ball will not run well) or an obstacle in the way. This shot will have more air time and less ground roll. Three-time Ryder Cup member Mark O'Meara offers the following suggestions for pitching shots softly onto the green. In getting the feel of your swing, "throw" the ball with your club — similar to throwing a softball. Your right hand will cause a high follow-through with the club — "almost at shoulder level"

that will cause a "release of the ball with an upward motion." Keep your knees flexed and let the weight shift to the left side as you follow through. Winner of both the U.S. Open and the Dinah Shore in 1975, Canadian Sandra Palmer also suggests shortening your grip 2-3 inches and opening your stance (or the face of the club). She also feels that slowing down your backswing will help achieve maximum acceleration.

A chip shot, where your approach "runs" after hitting the green, is called for when you have: a poor lie, a downhill lie, very much wind, or a hard green. This time your ball will have less hang-time in the air and more ground time on the green. "Snuggle up to the ball" — bringing your feet closer together for a crisp compact swing. As you address the ball, keep your hands opposite your left thigh and use more arms and less body action. Keep the blade of your club square to the target, and keep your hands ahead of or even with the clubhead at all times. O'Meara suggests this shot is more like a "toss of a ball with an almost side-arm action. There is no full upward follow-through and your hands should stop about waist high." On short wedge shots, Harvey Penick always taught that your backswing and follow-through is like "swinging a bucket of water without losing a drop."

On all short shots, Jack Nicklaus offers the following advice. Be slow and deliberate on short shots. "Be firm on your feet when playing pitch shots. If you watch the Tour players, you'll notice there is very little lifting of the heels on these short high-flying shots." Be certain to accelerate as you swing "THROUGH the ball not AT it." Nicklaus also suggests that from 20 yards out, use an 8 or 9 iron, but if you're closer (say 4-5 yards from the green), consider a less-lofted club like a 5 or 6 iron. Try both "an all-wrist action or a fairly stiff-wristed stroke" on short shots to see which works best for you.

Practice is the biggest key to success on your short shots. The beauty is you can practice in your own back yard. The greatest improvement you can make is getting the ball closer to the hole. The main goal is getting our ball in the cup.

Likewise, getting closer to God should be our first objective in life. Every other objective will be better fulfilled if we first draw close to Him. We will be better parents, better spouses, better students, better teachers, better you-name-it, if we will draw near to God. Our main goal, however, is being "in Christ" — or more appropriately, having Christ "in us."

Evangelist Luis Palau says, "Many Christians miss out on the thrill of Christian living because they have not understood that Jesus Christ literally lives within them." He uses a word-picture of a gloved hand. "The glove is a limp piece of leather until the hand moves into the glove and begins to mobilize it." The glove does not work on its own but through the hand inside. "In a sense," shares Palau, "Jesus' living in us is like the hand in the glove."

Are you allowing the hand of Christ to work inside your life?

[Jesus speaking] *"If a man remains in me and I in him, he will bear much fruit; apart from me you can do nothing"* (John 15:5).

"The closer your hands are to the clubhead, the greater your control and the more delicate your touch, so learn to choke down on the little shots."
— Jack Nicklaus

Lesson 26
Be Creative

In his book, *Strokes of Genius*, Thomas Bosell says, "The only bruises in golf are to the spirit . . . the only blood . . . internal hemorrhaging of self-esteem. Golf tests not so much the muscles as those qualities of stable judgment and emotional courage that reside between the ears."

Golf is a thinking person's game. We've all read recently about our ability to think with both the left side and right side of our brains. The left side is the analytical part where we set strategies and develop a mental toughness. The right side is the more creative, emotional, and imaginative side. Both sides are needed for success in golf. To visualize, we need to think about how we want to play a hole, but we also need to imagine it in our mind's eye.

Fred Couples believes Tom Watson to be "one of the finest strategists in golf." Five-time winner of the British Open where strategy is a must, Watson says, "Once on the course, try to forget mechanics and think tactics." He goes on to say that there is always a safe route and a more hazardous route to the hole. "The greater the risk, the greater the reward. To judge your risk/reward possibilities intelligently, you have to know your strengths and weaknesses. Play to your strengths and away from your weaknesses."

However, Tom Kite reminds us that you can't experience every shot ahead of time. "Imagination and creativity play a tremendous role," says Kite, especially "in recovering from trouble." Kite's mentor and coach, Harvey Penick always taught students to "play golf out of the creative side of your brain."

Bob Mann, in his *Automatic Golf* series, says we must use both sides of our brain, but he would agree with Penick that it is the creative side (or right side) that should take over on the course. Mann says it is helpful to understand the mechanics and physics of the game and to analyze how you want to play (with your left-brain). However, right-brained people (more often women) may have a better "feel" for the game. It is the right-brain that is more free-flowing and natural that will bring about the smooth and relaxed swing.

The right side of our brain, with this more free-flowing attitude is from where we get creativity for the arts — for painting and music and literature. It is also from where we can "spin" ideas. The "spin doctors" in political campaigns take anything about their opponent and put a "negative spin" on it.

We need to put a "positive spin" on our daily activities — to analyze situations and find creative solutions. Bill and Lindy Seltzer of Springfield, Illinois, were upset when the KKK held a rally in their town. They hesitated at causing any demonstrations that would only give the Klansmen more free publicity (often their goal anyway). Still they felt "doing nothing would let the racist message go unanswered." The Seltzers organized a pledge drive, like the walk-a-thons and read-a-thons and rock-a-thons used for charity causes. For every minute the rally lasted, you could pledge a dime or dollar or whatever amount you chose to be donated to an organization that opposed the KKK philosophy. "The idea was the longer the Klan rallied, the more they raised for the NAACP, the Anti-

Defamation League, and other groups that teach tolerance," said Bill Seltzer. They raised nearly $10,500 from the 45-minute duration of the rally. What a creative way to turn something negative into something positive!

God does not promise that our days will be filled with only goodness. Satan still controls much on earth. But, God can take anything and use it for our good if we will let Him work through us. Look for the positive possibilities in everything. We can turn hatred into love; sorrow into joy; fear into peace.

"And we know that in all things God works for the good of those who love him and who have been called according to his purpose" (Rom. 8:28).

"Your swing takes 1-1/2 to 2 seconds. You can't think your way through it. It must be smooth and natural." — Bob Mann

Lesson 27

Carry the Load

Born in 1957 in the poor Basque region of Spain, Seve Ballesteros learned to play the game of golf as a caddie. He loved "the rain in Spain" because that meant regulars would not be playing and he could use the time to practice. He shot a 79 at age 12, and ten years later would win the British Open. The following year he also won the 1980 Masters.

Many other professionals began their golfing careers in the caddy shack. Sam Snead, Byron Nelson, Ben Hogan, and Arnold Palmer are among former caddies with successful golf careers. In 1913, Francis Quimet (two-time U.S. Amateur Champion) won the U.S. Open as a 20-year-old amateur. The championship was held at Brookline, Massachusetts, where he was a caddie.

The word "caddie" comes from the French word, cadet. Mary, Queen of Scot, loved golf and used cadets to carry her clubs. These bag-toting caddies were barely given tips, whereas today's caddies make quite nice salaries on the PGA Tour.

The role of the caddie today goes well beyond just carrying the load. Caddies are expected to know the complete lay of the land including the exact yardage from every point on the course to the pin ahead. They attend the flagstick, make certain all the clubs are in the bag, and help select the correct club for their player. Some who have caddied for the same professional for many years even offer occasional advice. Ben Crenshaw was struggling during the 1995 Masters. His long-time caddie at Augusta

Payne Stewart
Perennial "Best Dressed"

National, Carl Jackson, suggested, "Put the ball a little back in your stance, Ben. And you got to turn your shoulders more." After only four practice balls, Crenshaw's swing was suddenly back again. Said Crenshaw, "I've never had a confidence transformation like that in my life."

Many players have close relationships with their caddie. Some golfers have even used relatives. Kelli Kuehne, 1995 U.S. Amateur Champion, used her brother, Trip, who lost the Men's Amateur earlier in the season to Tiger Woods. Woods had used his sports psychologist, Jay Brunza, as caddie for five USGA championships. It's not unusual for friends from the amateur ranks to caddie for one another in big tournaments if one fails to make the cut. With the use of pull-carts, most caddies in Japan are women except at the top professional level. Mashiro Kuramoto says it is considered an honor for a man to caddie for another man. Jim Gallagher Jr. considers it an honor to have Al Hansen serve as his caddie. He also considers him a friend. When Gallagher accepted Christ, he phoned Hansen who lived in Las Vegas. "He was so pumped up, he wanted to hug me from there," said Gallagher.

That is the way we should all feel when someone we know accepts Christ. Until they do, we can carry their load — both in prayer and caring service. As a Christian caddie, we may be called on to point the way, offer some friendly advice, and perhaps just stand by silently, or maybe they just need a hug.

In his book, *Stretcher Bearers,* Michael Slater talks about the popular song. "They'll Know We Are Christians by Our Love, by Our Love." He says that we know all the right phrases to use, but he chastens, "Do we live out the message of the song and these phrases?" Slater reminds us that "Christianity is more than just going to church. Christianity," he says, "is that intimate relationship with Him lived out among one another."

In living among those who are either struggling with some burden or celebrating their redemption in Christ, we can offer the hugs He cannot give from heaven. As Christian speaker Joan Mayers often said we can be "Jesus with skin on" to others.

"Carry each other's burdens, and in this way you will be fulfilling the law of Christ" (Gal. 6:2).

[To caddie Jerry Beard]: "I've been like a blind man with a seeing-eye dog all week. You sure enough got me here. Just read me one more putt." — Fuzzy Zoeller (on the 18th green at Augusta National on 4/16/79 for his first Masters' victory)

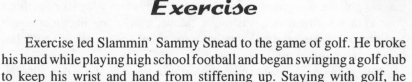

Lesson 28
Exercise

Exercise led Slammin' Sammy Snead to the game of golf. He broke his hand while playing high school football and began swinging a golf club to keep his wrist and hand from stiffening up. Staying with golf, he developed one of the sweetest golf swings in the history of the game.

A golf swing uses nearly every muscle in the body, and walking is one of the easiest and best exercises for a healthy body. No wonder golf is accepted as one of the most well-rounded forms of exercise.

The opposite is also true. To become a good golfer, you must prepare through exercise. "You can have all the talent in the world," says Nancy Lopez, "but if your body is in bad shape, you won't be able to get the most out of your game."

Walking, riding bicycles (stationery or outdoors), and using treadmills or small trampolines are good for the cardiovascular (circulatory) system and also help get your body in shape for the walking you will face on the golf course. Since the legs provide the real power for your golf swing, you may also want to include isometrics (the use of weights or resistance) as another form of exercise to strengthen legs and other specific areas of the body. Don't forget stretching exercises especially for your back and hamstrings. Toe touches (standing or sitting), leg lifts, and squats are all simple stretching techniques.

Hand and forearm exercises are often overlooked, but can improve your golf score dramatically. Squeeze a hand grip or soft rubber ball while you watch TV or drive the car. Gardening is another way to get good exercise for the hands. Work more with your weaker hand. For right-handed golfers, use your left hand in small ways everyday like brushing your teeth, opening doors, washing windows, etc. Improving the strength and "touch" of this hand and arm that act as the extension of your golf club is extremely important.

Bob Mann teaches what he calls the "motor move." Grip the golf club with the three fingers of your left hand only and swing back and forth like a pendulum — eventually swinging a full arc. This not only strengthens the left arm and hand but develops your golf swing at the same time.

Learning some relaxation exercises can also be valuable for both golf and life. Deep-breathing, neck rolls, limp hand shaking, and other simple techniques are but a few ways to release tension in your body. You can try these walking from the tee to your second shot or while waiting to putt on the green (provided that you are not in sight of another player and causing a distraction).

To ease the tension in a busy work day, take a few minutes and walk down the hall, look out the window, and take a deep breath. When you return to your desk, you'll be amazed how much fresher your ideas are for the task at hand. When the kids are driving you positively nuts, taking a walk outdoors for some fresh air and a change of scenery can be the break you all need.

Walking with God is the best way to relieve tension and get back on track, but God often wants us to exercise our faith in other ways. He may call us to "stretch" ourselves — to move out of our normal daily routines and become involved with new adventures and missions. This "stretching" means getting out of our "comfort zones." Father John Powell says, "These comfort zones apply to the way we dress, the emotions we can comfortably express, the things which we will try, the depths to which we reveal ourselves, our openness to change, and so forth." Stretching means we "expand our awareness . . . we do something right and reasonable, which we have always felt inhibited from trying." Powell says this need not be a giant step. Keep in mind, the results could be discouraging. We might even have to apologize. But, according to Powell, "Stretching means a fuller life and a larger world."

Powell says if we never step out of our comfort zone, he can already predict how our life will end — just like it is now, "only more so." However, if we stretch, no one can predict our future. "The sky is the limit."

"Observe the command of the Lord, walking in his ways and revering him" (Deut. 8:6).

"I have three basic beliefs: faith in God, value of education, and good physical fitness." — Gary Player, when asked why he is so successful

Lesson 29
On the Green

Constantino Rocca sank an unbelievable 65-foot putt rolling up and down the undulating green of the 18th hole at St. Andrews to tie John Daly after regulation play in the 1995 British Open. Who would have imagined that to win the 4-hole play-off, Daly (better known for his long drives) would come back with a 35-foot birdie putt of his own!

Putting is the most personal part of the game of golf. Some of the newer, longer putters require a radically different grip. With the more standard putters, most golfers maintain the same grip they use for drives and short shots. Nancy Lopez, Seve Ballesteros, and others keep their same basic grip, but extend the right index finger down the shaft of the putter. A few others change their putting grip, like Arnold Palmer who actually maintains some space between his hands on the grip of his putter.

The putting stance is perfectly square to the hole, and the stroke is a smooth, even flow using only the shoulders and arms. There is no wrist movement and your hands stay ahead of the clubhead all the way through. The key of all good putters is maintaining the same distance in the take-away and the follow-through. Seve Ballesteros describes it as "keeping a perfect pendulum action, with the clubhead moving backward and forward the same distance, at the same speed, at the same height over the turf."

High handicappers should use the putter even off the green whenever possible. Jack Nicklaus uses the "Texas Wedge" — a shot from off the green — putting the ball instead of chipping or pitching it — anytime conditions allow. These are generally when the turf is firm and dry and fairly even. To play this shot, Nicklaus says to strike the ball a little harder than normal and "keep your head and body perfectly still!"

Practice these shots around the practice green, which is the most valuable area of the golf course to beginners. The more you practice your putting, the more confidence you gain and the faster your scores will go down.

Palmer, one of the best putters on tour, says four main conditions affect your putt: slope, texture of the green, grain, and wind. Obviously, you have to stroke the ball harder if you are hitting into the wind, and the wind behind you will help carry a putt faster. Some say the grain always runs toward the east, toward any nearby valley, or toward water. You can best judge the grain by looking down at the turf's "sheen." A shiny appearance between your ball and the cup means you are putting down grain; a dull look is into the grain. Putts running down grain will run faster and into (or against) the grain more slowly. The texture of the grain also affects the speed of the ball. A wet surface will play more slowly than a dry solid green.

The slope plays the most important role in "reading your putt." The naked eye can tell you a lot as you approach the green. "Eyeball the green — like looking at the horizon," says Palmer. Build a computer "break bank" in your memory of holes and their slopes so when you play them the next time, you already have the information at hand. Watch how other players' balls break.

The most common method for reading the slope is the "plumb bob" you have seen many golfers use. Holding your putter with the fingertips of one hand at arm's length in front of you, stand (or squat) over your ball's location, close one eye and look straight at the hole. If the hole falls on the left side of the shaft, the slope breaks left to right (and vice versa).

While building a new church, Pastor Fred Shaw found an old plumb bob made from a stone tied around a string. He showed how the weight of the stone pulls toward the center of gravity, causing an exact perpendicular line to the face of the earth. He explained how this measure was used in olden days to show the vertical standard for buildings. Pastor Shaw further explained how the Lord used a similar plumb line in the days of Amos, the minor prophet. Just like today, God warned His people needed to stand true against His measure. "We need to remember that we are not better than anyone else because we are Christians," says Pastor Shaw. "We only have a better standard."

Who or what is your standard? Do you measure your life against the plumb line of God's Word?

"Then the Lord said, 'Look I am setting a plumb line among my people' " (Amos 7:8).

"A tap in of half an inch counts the same as a drive of 280 yards." — Arnold Palmer.

Lesson 30
In the Present

"You can't play the next shot until you have played this one." That may sound like a Yogi Berra quote, but credit it to golf instructor Mary Lena Faulk. When asked what one piece of advice she would give to golfers, regardless of their age, sex, physique, and ability, Faulk replied, "Remember the game is played one stroke at a time."

With seven wins in his first six years on the PGA Tour, Lee Janzen had the best record since Johnny Miller won 11 events in his first six seasons. Janzen says that staying focused is a key for him. His sports psychologist, Dr. Deborah Graham, believes it is this ability that allows Janzen to "deal with problems as they arise." He follows her motto: "The past does not equal the future." If you make a mistake, put it behind you and focus on the problem at hand.

Jack Nicklaus offers similar advice: "Blank out bad shots." He consciously forces himself to focus immediately on the recovery shot he needs to make. He says, "I switch off of fault and on to remedy as fast as I possibly can."

Tom Kite says, "The error I see a lot of amateurs making is trying to get too much out of every shot." If you don't play low shots very well, then don't expect to miraculously play a perfect shot from behind the trees. "Don't worry so much about getting to the green until you're out from behind the tree." If you try too much, you may still be behind the tree — or worse. You have to avoid the immediate obstacle.

The immediate shot is the only one that counts. "A golf swing happens now — not in the past, not in the future," says Harvey Penick. Nancy Lopez concurs. "You need to focus on each shot, one shot at a time. You can't get too high or too low about the previous shot or hole. And you can't worry about what's going to happen two holes from now. You have to live in the present on the course."

Sounds like good advice for all of us whether golfers or not. We need to learn the secret of living in the "now."

It's okay to remember the past, and it's a good idea to plan for the future, but we must live in the present. "Whatever we have done in the past, be it good or evil, great or small, is irrelevant to our stance before God today," say Brennan Manning in his stories of *The Ragamuffin Gospel*. He continues, "Whatever past achievements might bring us honor, whatever past disgraces might make us blush, all have been crucified with Christ and exist no more except in the deep recesses of eternity." He reminds us, "It is only *now* that we are in the presence of God."

Remember your blessings. Look with enthusiasm toward the future. But live in His presence today — right now!

"Give us today our daily bread" (Matt. 6:11).

"Do your best with what you've got today, and do it one shot at a time." — Mary Lena Faulk (winner of the US Amateur, several professional events, and long-time teacher of golf at Broadmoor)

Sources and Recommended Reading

In accordance with copyright laws, all quotes are brief enough in nature and not in competition with any of the following texts and sources that written permission was not necessary. However, we do wish to acknowledge these authors and individuals and encourage you to purchase the books, etc. for further reading.

"Arnie Fan Shares Lead," *The Cincinnati Enquirer,* 6/30/95.

Auch, Ron, *The Heart of the King* (Green Forest, AR: New Leaf Press, Inc., 1995).

Brett Avery, editor, "A Historic Retrospective," *Golf Journal,* June 1995.

Azinger, Paul with Ken Abraham, *Zinger* (Grand Rapids, MI: Zondervan Publishing House, 1995).

Bamberger, Michael, "Par for the Course," *Sports Illustrated,* 11/6/95.

Benson, Bob, *He Speaks Softly* (Waco, TX: Word Books, 1985).

Benson, Peggy, *Listen For a God Who Whispers* (Nashville, TN: Celebration Press, 1991), (reprinted by Vaughan Printing, 1994).

Benz, Rob, "Making the Turn," *Sports Spectrum,* July 1995.

Boswell, Thomas, *Strokes of Genius* (Garden City, NY: Doubleday & Co., Inc., 1987).

Bryant, Brad, "Finding Your Game," Taylor-Made commercial (see "Fire & Ice").

Campbell, Malcolm, *The Random House International Encyclopedia of Golf* (New York, NY: Random House, 1991).

"Check the Clock for a Better Grip," *Golf Digest,* October 1995.

"Chip 'n' a Putt Net $150,000," *The Cincinnati Enquirer,* Cincinnati, OH, 11/26/95.

Coyne, John, editor, *The New Golf for Women* (New York, NY: A Rutledge Book by Doubleday & Co., Inc., 1973).

Daughtery, Paul, "Can't Help Loving Masters," *The Cincinnati Enquirer,* Cincinnati, OH, 4/6/95.

Daughtery, Paul, "Crenshaw Must've Played His Heart Out" *The Cincinnati Enquirer,* Cincinnati, OH, 4/10/95.

Dunaway, James C, "Mail Ministerial Burnout" (a doctoral project) (Dayton, OH: United Theological Seminary, April 1987).

Enger, David, "You're New Here, Aren't You?" *Sports Spectrum,* May 1994.

Faldo, Nick (with John Huggan), "How to Stop the Bleeding," *Golf Digest,* May 1995.

Feinstein, John, *A Good Walk Spoiled* (Boston, MA: Little, Brown and Co., Ltd., 1995).

"Fire and Ice — the 1996 PGA Tour," hosted by Dick Enberg for NBC television (PGA Tours Productions), 1/13/96.

Flynn, Beverly, "This Is Wondrous Strange!" *Sports Spectrum*, May 1994.

Floyd, Raymond with Guy Yocum, "My Slump-Busting Putting Keys*," Golf Digest*, July 1995.

Foulke, Karen, "Hawaiian Honeymoon," *Sports Spectrum*, October 1995.

Foulke, Karen, "Partners for the Course," *Sports Spectrum*, June 1995.

Geiberger, Al, "Neuromuscular Training GOLF" (audio-video tapes) (Newark, CA: SyberVision Systems, Inc., 1986).

Glenn, Rhonda, *The Illustrated History of Women's Golf* (Dallas, TX: Taylor Publishing Co., 1991).

God's Treasury of Virtues (Tulsa, OK: Honor Books, 1995).

GOLF: More About Sports/Features @ Prodigy, 1995-96.

Goldman, Michael, "Cheating Destroys Character," *The Cincinnati Enquirer*, Cincinnati, OH, 1/7/96.

GolfWeb Library, Paul Conrad, moderator, "Library & Reference," Cupertino, CA: Prodigy, 1994-96.

Hansel, Tim, *When I Relax, I Feel Guilty* (Elgin, IL: David C. Cook Publishing, Co., 1979).

"The Inaugural Rolex Challenge," ESPN, Bristol, CT, (tape played) 12/27/95.

Inside the PGA Tour, "The Year in Review," PGA Tour Productions, ESPN, 1/6/96.

Kite, Tom and Larry Dennis, *How to Play Consistent Golf* (Trumbull, CT: Pocket Book, Golf Digest, 1990).

Klug, Ronald, *How to Keep a Spiritual Journal* (Nashville, TN: Thomas Nelson Publishers, 1982).

Lawrence, Brother, *The Practice of the Presence of God* (Grand Rapids, MI: Fleming H. Revell, 1958).

Liebman, Glenn, *Golf Shorts* (Chicago, IL: Contemporary Books, Inc., 1995).

Lopez, Nancy with Don Wade, *Nancy Lopez's the Complete Golfer* (Chicago, IL: Contemporary Books, Inc., 1987).

MacDonald, Bob and Les Bolstad, *How to Improve Your Golf* (Chicago, IL: National Golf Foundation, 1962).

Mackey, Richard T, *GOLF: Learn Thru Auditory and Visual Cues* (Dubuque, IA: Kendall/Hunt Publishing Co., 1975).

Mann, Bob, "Automatic Golf — Let's Get Started" video (Malibu, CA: Bob Mann Sports, 1990).

Mann, Bob, "Automatic Golf — the Method" video (Malibu, CA: Bob Mann Sports, 1990).

Manning, Brennan, *The Ragamuffin Gospel* (Portland, OR: Multnomah Press, 1990).

McLean, Jim with Larry Dennis, *Golf Digest Book of Drills* (New York, NY: Pocket Books, Simon & Schuster, Inc., 1990).

Flynn, Beverly, "This Is Wondrous Strange!" *Sports Spectrum*, May 1994.

Floyd, Raymond with Guy Yocum, "My Slump-Busting Putting Keys*," Golf Digest*, July 1995.

Foulke, Karen, "Hawaiian Honeymoon," *Sports Spectrum*, October 1995.

Foulke, Karen, "Partners for the Course," *Sports Spectrum*, June 1995.

Geiberger, Al, "Neuromuscular Training GOLF" (audio-video tapes) (Newark, CA: SyberVision Systems, Inc., 1986).

Glenn, Rhonda, *The Illustrated History of Women's Golf* (Dallas, TX: Taylor Publishing Co., 1991).

God's Treasury of Virtues (Tulsa, OK: Honor Books, 1995).

GOLF: More About Sports/Features @ Prodigy, 1995-96.

Goldman, Michael, "Cheating Destroys Character," *The Cincinnati Enquirer*, Cincinnati, OH, 1/7/96.

GolfWeb Library, Paul Conrad, moderator, "Library & Reference," Cupertino, CA: Prodigy, 1994-96.

Hansel, Tim, *When I Relax, I Feel Guilty* (Elgin, IL: David C. Cook Publishing, Co., 1979).

"The Inaugural Rolex Challenge," ESPN, Bristol, CT, (tape played) 12/27/95.

Inside the PGA Tour, "The Year in Review," PGA Tour Productions, ESPN, 1/6/96.

Kite, Tom and Larry Dennis, *How to Play Consistent Golf* (Trumbull, CT: Pocket Book, Golf Digest, 1990).

Klug, Ronald, *How to Keep a Spiritual Journal* (Nashville, TN: Thomas Nelson Publishers, 1982).

Lawrence, Brother, *The Practice of the Presence of God* (Grand Rapids, MI: Fleming H. Revell, 1958).

Liebman, Glenn, *Golf Shorts* (Chicago, IL: Contemporary Books, Inc., 1995).

Lopez, Nancy with Don Wade, *Nancy Lopez's the Complete Golfer* (Chicago, IL: Contemporary Books, Inc., 1987).

MacDonald, Bob and Les Bolstad, *How to Improve Your Golf* (Chicago, IL: National Golf Foundation, 1962).

Mackey, Richard T, *GOLF: Learn Thru Auditory and Visual Cues* (Dubuque, IA: Kendall/Hunt Publishing Co., 1975).

Mann, Bob, "Automatic Golf — Let's Get Started" video (Malibu, CA: Bob Mann Sports, 1990).

Mann, Bob, "Automatic Golf — the Method" video (Malibu, CA: Bob Mann Sports, 1990).

Manning, Brennan, *The Ragamuffin Gospel* (Portland, OR: Multnomah Press, 1990).

McLean, Jim with Larry Dennis, *Golf Digest Book of Drills* (New York, NY: Pocket Books, Simon & Schuster, Inc., 1990).

Sources and Recommended Reading

In accordance with copyright laws, all quotes are brief enough in nature and not in competition with any of the following texts and sources that written permission was not necessary. However, we do wish to acknowledge these authors and individuals and encourage you to purchase the books, etc. for further reading.

"Arnie Fan Shares Lead," *The Cincinnati Enquirer,* 6/30/95.

Auch, Ron, *The Heart of the King* (Green Forest, AR: New Leaf Press, Inc., 1995).

Brett Avery, editor, "A Historic Retrospective," *Golf Journal*, June 1995.

Azinger, Paul with Ken Abraham, *Zinger* (Grand Rapids, MI: Zondervan Publishing House, 1995).

Bamberger, Michael, "Par for the Course," *Sports Illustrated*, 11/6/95.

Benson, Bob, *He Speaks Softly* (Waco, TX: Word Books, 1985).

Benson, Peggy, *Listen For a God Who Whispers* (Nashville, TN: Celebration Press, 1991), (reprinted by Vaughan Printing, 1994).

Benz, Rob, "Making the Turn," *Sports Spectrum*, July 1995.

Boswell, Thomas, *Strokes of Genius* (Garden City, NY: Doubleday & Co., Inc., 1987).

Bryant, Brad, "Finding Your Game," Taylor-Made commercial (see "Fire & Ice").

Campbell, Malcolm, *The Random House International Encyclopedia of Golf* (New York, NY: Random House, 1991).

"Check the Clock for a Better Grip," *Golf Digest*, October 1995.

"Chip 'n' a Putt Net $150,000," *The Cincinnati Enquirer,* Cincinnati, OH, 11/26/95.

Coyne, John, editor, *The New Golf for Women* (New York, NY: A Rutledge Book by Doubleday & Co., Inc., 1973).

Daughtery, Paul, "Can't Help Loving Masters," *The Cincinnati Enquirer*, Cincinnati, OH, 4/6/95.

Daughtery, Paul, "Crenshaw Must've Played His Heart Out*" The Cincinnati Enquirer,* Cincinnati, OH, 4/10/95.

Dunaway, James C, "Mail Ministerial Burnout" (a doctoral project) (Dayton, OH: United Theological Seminary, April 1987).

Enger, David, "You're New Here, Aren't You?" *Sports Spectrum,* May 1994.

Faldo, Nick (with John Huggan), "How to Stop the Bleeding," *Golf Digest*, May 1995.

Feinstein, John, *A Good Walk Spoiled* (Boston, MA: Little, Brown and Co., Ltd., 1995).

"Fire and Ice — the 1996 PGA Tour," hosted by Dick Enberg for NBC television (PGA Tours Productions), 1/13/96.

Meacham, Gary, "Bill of Rights," *Sports Spectrum,* December 1995.

Meserole, Mike, editor, *The 1995 Information Please Sports Almanac* (Boston, MA: Houghton Mifflin Company, 1995).

Nicklaus, Jack with Ken Bowden, *Play Better Golf — the Short Game and Scoring* (New York, NY: Pocket Books, Simon & Schuster, Inc., 1981).

Nicklaus, Jack with Ken Bowden, *Play Better Golf — the Swing from A-Z* (New York, NY: Pocket Books, Simon & Schuster, Inc., 1980).

Ogilvie, Lloyd John, *Silent Strength for My Life* (Eugene, OR: Harvey House Publishers, 1990).

O'Meara, Mark with Mike Stachura, "Recapture Your Feel," *Golf Digest*, August 1995.

Palmer, Arnold and Peter Dobereiner, *Arnold Palmer's Complete Book of Putting* (New York, NY: Atheneum, 1986).

Palau, Luis, "The Indwelling Christ," *Practical Christianity* (Wheaton, IL: Tyndale House Publishers, Inc., 1987).

Palmeri, Allen, "Going Public," *Sports Spectrum,* June 1994.

Pavin, Corey with John Huggan, "How to Shape Your Shots," *Golf Digest*, August 1995.

Penick, Harvey with Bud Shrake, *For All Who Love the Game — Lessons & Teachings for Women* (New York, NY: Simon & Schuster, 1995).

Penick, Harvey with Bud Shrake, *Harvey Penick's Little Red Book* (New York, NY: Simon & Schuster, 1992).

Penick, Harvey with Bud Shrake, *If You Play Golf, You're My Friend* (New York, NY: Simon & Schuster, 1993).

PGA Tour — Official Media Guide (Chicago, IL: Triumph Books, 1994).

Player, Gary with Desmond Tolhurst, *Golf Begins at Fifty — Play the Lifetime Game Better then Ever* (New York, NY: Simon & Schuster, 1988).

Powell, John, S.J., *Through Seasons of the Heart,* July 22 & 23 (Allen, TX: Tabor Publishing, 1987).

Precker, Michael, "Couple Turns Klan on Its Pointed Head" (Dallas Morning News), *The Cincinnati Enquirer*, 1/1/96.

Reilly, Rick, "Another World," *Sports Illustrated*, 12/11/95.

Reilly, Rick, "An Epic Finish," *Sports Illustrated*, 7/31/95.

Reilly, Rick, "For You, Harvey," *Sports Illustrated*, 4/17/95.

Reilly, Rick, "Goodness Gracious, He's a Great Ball of Fire," *Sports Illustrated*, 3/27/95.

Reilly, Rick, "Road Test," *Sports Illustrated*, 7/24/95.

Reilly, Rick, "The Rock," *Sports Illustrated*, 9/25/95.

Reilly, Rick, "Wrong Man, Wrong Time," *Sports Illustrated*, 10/2/95.

"Ryder Captain Kite May Play, Too," *The Cincinnati Enquirer*, 1995.

Rosaforte, Tim, "The Comeback Kid," *Sports Illustrated*, 9/5/94.

Sandrolini, Mark, "Working-Class King," *Sports Spectrum*, December 1995.

Schuller, Robert H., *Tough Times Never Last, But Tough People Do!* (Nashville, TN: Thomas Nelson Publishing, 1983).

"The Senior PGA Tour," PGA Tour Productions, ESPN, 1/6/96.

"Selling out St. Andrews," *Sports Illustrated*, 12/4/95.

Shaw, Fred, "The Plumb Line for Building a New Life," Trinity United Methodist Church, Milford, OH, 7/16/95.

Shaw, Fred, "The Making of a Saint," 10/29/95.

Slater, Michael, *Stretcher Bearers* (Ventura, CA: Regal Books, GL Publications, 1975).

Strand, Robert, *Moments for Grandparents* (Green Forest, AR: New Leaf Press, Inc., 1994).

Swindoll, Charles R., *Growing Strong in the Seasons of Life* (Portland, OR: Multnomah Press, 1983).

Swindoll, Charles R., *Strengthening Your Grip* (Waco, TX: Word Books, 1982).

Tarde, Jerry, editor, "Cool Madness in the Heat of Summer," *Golf Digest*, November 1995.

Tarde, Jerry, "Superwoman-in-Waiting," *Golf Digest*, August 1995.

"They Call Him the Closer," *Golf Digest*, November 1995.

VanKempen, Kenneth, *Visual Golf* (New York, NY: Simon & Schuster, 1992).

"Waddy's' World," *Sports Spectrum*, December 1993.

Walk to Emmaus, "Discipleship" Talk (Nashville, TN: The Upper Room, 1985).

Watson, Tom with Nick Seitz, *Tom Watson's Strategic Golf* (New York, NY: Pocket Books, 1993).

Williams, Pat, with Bill Bright, editor, *The Greatest Lesson I've Ever Learned* (San Bernardino, CA: Here's Life Publishers, 1991).

Woolwine, Sam, "Two Strokes BACK — Three Steps FORWARD," *Sports Spectrum*, August 1994.

The World Book Encyclopedia (Chicago, IL: World Book, Inc., 1983), vol. 8-G.

World Championship of Golf, ABC Sports, New York, NY (from Scottsdale, AZ), 12/31/95.

Wright, H. Norman, *How to Have a Creative Crisis* (Dallas, TX: Word Publishing, 1986).

If you are interested in learning golf Harvey Penick's way, a complete golf complex and school has been built. For information contact: Harvey Penick Golf Academy, Goldsmith International, Austin, Texas, 1-800-477-5869.